UP, UP
and OVER

HERB HIRATA

Order this book online at www.trafford.com
or email orders@trafford.com

Most Trafford titles are also available at major online book retailers.

Printed in the United States of America.

ISBN: 978-1-4907-5195-5 (sc)
ISBN: 978-1-4907-5196-2 (hc)
ISBN: 978-1-4907-5197-9 (e)

Library of Congress Control Number: 2014921453

Trafford rev. 12/05/2014

 www.trafford.com

North America & international
toll-free: 1 888 232 4444 (USA & Canada)
fax: 812 355 4082

To all the Forward Air Controllers
Who flew Cessna 02A aircraft in combat.
Thank you for your kindness and
Acceptance of navigators into your elite
Program.

CONTENTS

INTRODUCTION

Two neat stacks of National Geographic Magazines stored in a corner. Too nice, too expensive to be thrown out with the garbage. They contained hidden treasures to be read and admired, to make one wonder: Will I ever see any of these areas in my lifetime? They both provoked me and inspired me to find a way out of the coffee fields of Kona, Hawaii. To fulfill my dream of seeing the entire United States, from the Golden Gate Bridge to the Statue of Liberty. To see the Rocky Mountains, golden fields of corn, vast prairie lands, Old Faithful erupting, Mount Rushmore, Dodge City, the OK Corral, Plymouth Rock, the Shenandoah Valley, Kitty Hawk where the Wright Brothers flew, drink from Ponce de Leon's Fountain of Youth, see Stephen Foster's Swanee River, Bourbon Street, the Alamo, Sutter's Fort and of course, the Grand Canyon. Maybe a glimpse of Hoover Dam and Las Vegas.

A lifetime of places to visit. I never dreamed that I would fulfill most of my journey by age 30.

From hearing the bombs drop on Pearl Harbor as a child in 1941 to flying at Mach 1, 200 feet over the ground, following the road leading north into Dien Bien Phu, route pack 5, North Vietnam, 1968, this is my story this is my life.

CHAPTER ONE

Dien Bien Phu

As I grow older, it becomes increasingly harder to remember events that happened so long ago. Sometimes pictures, movies or people will jog my memory and I will recall specific events.

In the middle of a reconnaissance mission over North Vietnam, an amazing occurrence happened. Time stopped for me and I stepped back into my past. 2 Minutes of vivid images of my last 30 of living passed through my mind in slow motion. Memories that were stored in the back of my brain came to life.

Now, 46 years later, I still remember those early images as if I were still there. They started with the bombing of Pearl Harbor in 1941 and ended with the pilot saying: "It's over, let's get out of here!"

A.   A RECONNAISSANCE MISSION

On a sunny day in January, 1968, we took off from Udorn Air Force Base, northeast Thailand in an RF-4C reconnaissance fighter. We headed northwest over Laos as a deceptive measure flying at a moderate speed and altitude. Bright sunlight flooded through the clear canopy above us. The aircraft air conditioning was on but it didn't take long for our flight suits to become soaked with sweat.

Our mission: Take aerial photographs of the current gun employments, missile sites, supplies and forces the North Vietnamese military had in the town of Dien Bien Phu, North Vietnam.

Escorted by 2-105 fighters, we proceeded northwest toward the Laotian, North Vietnamese, Chinese border. The RF-4C is a reconnaissance only version of the F-4 fighter. No guns, no weapons to fire. No- "C'mon, make my day" or "My guns are bigger than yours, wanna see?" moments.

The pilot flew the aircraft, I sat behind him and operated the cameras as well as navigated. On this day, the ground crew loaded 2 forward looking cameras in the nose and a sweeping, panoramic camera below me.

Not far from the Laotian-Chinese border, we dropped down to several hundred above the tree tops, below any enemy radar coverage and turned due east toward North Vietnam. Everything was now moving faster, including our apprehensions as we approached the ridge line separating Laos from North Vietnam. The fighter escort pulled off to wait for us.

We did a fast pop-up over the ridge, then immediately wings over and dive to the right turning 270 degrees from heading due east to due north. I positioned my left hand on the camera switches and my body twisted to the right looking over my right shoulder to watch the wing man cross over. The positive 5 "G" forces pushed me all the way down into the ejection seat. Couldn't move or speak until we finally rolled out heading north several hundred above the road leading into the town. The pilot accelerated to mach 1 speed (approximately 600-700 mph) and I turned the cameras on. We were now on a 3 minute run up the road leading into the town. Unlike propeller driven aircraft, the fighter cockpit is very quiet. You could hear yourself breathing but not the engines.

I relaxed for a few seconds to look out at what we had gotten into. There were twinkling lights all over the place. Wow! Beautiful! We're flying into a town at night. The villagers must be having a religious ceremony using candles, flashlights and torches.

All of a sudden, it dawned on me,.......It was daylight, not night! The lights twinkling were gun flashes from everyone and their cousin.... Firing at us! Oh God, we could crash and burn right now if they hit us. The North Vietnamese had lots of weapons. AK-47 rifles, howitzers, quad 50 mm caliber machine guns, RPG hand held rocket launchers (Russian and American), Russian 82 mm mortar launchers, anti-aircraft machine guns, 37 mm and 55 mm cannons, radar tracking mobile SAM missile launchers and even stones to throw.

My body froze, I became very scared and started to shake. Then a strange thing happened…. I became very calm. It was very quiet, eerily quiet, the silence was deafening. It felt like I was in a clear bubble looking out. Nothing could touch me. My last 30 years of living began to pass through my mind.

B.   GLIMPSES

Glimpses of events appeared in vivid color: Hearing the sounds of bombs exploding on Pearl Harbor on December 7, 1941 during the Japanese air attack on the Pacific Fleet, looking down into a huge cauldron of red hot liquid rocks, walking up to a river of lava flowing to the sea, feeling the earth tremble during a strong earthquake, sitting in an elementary school library reading all afternoon, marching down the streets of Honolulu in a May Day Parade, racing a herd of buffalo in South Dakota with my old Buick, sitting at the kitchen table in San Francisco helping my aunt Lily make sushi, closing my eyes and hanging on tight as I rode with my uncle James as he went blasting up and down the hilly streets of San Francisco, going to Winter Survival School, escaping from a simulated POW camp and running for the mountains above Reno, sleeping in a hollowed out log as the temperatures dropped below freezing, waiting for the newest B52-H being built to arrive at Homestead Air Force Base, Florida, fishing off the bridges on US1 leading to Key West, watching alligators and birds in the Everglades, ferrying a C-47 airplane across the Atlantic to France.

Too many images to describe in one chapter.

After an eternity, the run was over. We pulled straight up and headed for home. Relax….We're safe today. Tomorrow comes another mission, maybe it will be an easy one over route pack 1 or route pack 2.

The mission was over but the images remained in my mind.

CHAPTER TWO

Growing Up in Hawaii

A.   EARLY CHILDHOOD

As a child, I wondered about everything. What were those loud noises? Our parents moving around agitated, scared and worried. We lived in Kona, 200 miles southeast of Pearl Harbor with only open ocean between us. We heard distant booms early in the morning of December 7, 1941 as the Japanese attacked the Pacific Fleet with a surprise air attack. Two hours of continuous bombing. Our parents made lots of phone calls, covered all the windows with blankets and sheets. Everyone went to bed early, no lights. I was only 4 years old.

More than 2400 Americans were killed, 21 ships sunk or damaged and at least 188 American aircraft destroyed. We declared war on Japan the next day. Hawaii was placed under martial law with curfews, blackouts, gas rationing.

Around 150,000 people in Hawaii were Americans of Japanese descent, 40% of the population. Unlike California and other western states, internment for that many people was considered not very practical. We were allowed to live under martial law provided we tippy-toed and kept quiet. To a much lesser degree, Americans of German and Italian descent were treated with the same attitude.

Yes, World War II had started. Lots of talking about gas rationing. Actually, bitching and moaning. Other than the problems engendered by war, all I remember about being 4 years old is sitting outside with my sister Elaine mixing white lard with a packet of yellow food coloring to be used as simulated butter. It was Yuck!

In February 1943, the 442nd Infantry Regimental Combat Team was formed with volunteers from Americans of Japanese descent. Most of the volunteers were from Hawaii. They became our proud heritage. My uncle Mike and cousin Paul volunteered as well as many of my dad's friends. Being a school principal, dad decided that he could better serve by staying behind and was later exempted from the draft.

The 442nd trained in Louisiana and was sent to Europe. They fought mainly in Italy and France. They fought valiantly at the "Battle of the Bulge ". They are considered to be the most decorated infantry regiment in the history of the United States Army. Awards include 8 Presidential Unit Citations and 21 Congressional Medals of Honor. Their battle cry was: "Go for Broke!"

During a period of distrust, they made us proud to be Americans of Japanese descent. We were loyal Americans, nothing else.

Wondering about everything sometimes got me into trouble. Mom hired a nanny to care for us while they taught school during the day. She turned her back to us when she washed the dishes. I wondered what it was like to creep up on her from behind and see what was under those long dresses that she wore. The first few times were ok but it was fun so I continued. She quit—I was spanked hard with much yelling. Didn't know that mother knew cuss words.

Sister Elaine never got into trouble. I wondered what would happen if she started yelling and screaming so I bit her on the leg. Boy, was there a lot of yelling and screaming and not only by my sister but mom threw in some cuss words too. Sister got to stay in the house while I was put outside. Lesson in life #1—girls get all the breaks. They are just as strong and mean as us but maybe it's because they are considered prettier than boys.

I was allowed to play on a small dirt road that went past our front steps. It was flat until reaching some trees, then it sloped downhill. Instructed to only play up to the trees, I wondered what lay beyond the trees. One day, I inched slowly past the trees and got lost in some bushes. Punished for that too but to this day, some 70+ years later, I still always wonder what lies beyond the trees.

For the next 3-4 years, not much happened. We moved to another, larger elementary school with dad as the principal and mother teaching. In August, 1945, dad assembled everyone outside in the yard and made an announcement. I was a little late getting there, saw everyone jumping up and down, clapping loudly. It must be a school exercise so I joined in. It's fun jumping up and down, clapping your hands over your head and smiling at everyone. Of course, the war finally came to an end. Uncle Mike and Cousin Paul were coming home along with dad's friends.

There were quiet re-unions with families. The returning soldiers didn't say much about the war, they just tried to forget it. Today we call it post-traumatic stress and returning warriors get medical help and counseling. Back then, they drank and brooded.

My wondering turned to learning. Dad kept around 6-8 ducks in a closed pen. The land-sea effect of living 1500 feet in elevation, on the side of a mountain created rain on most afternoons. The ground in the duck pen was always somewhat muddy with a few dry spots. I learned how to survey the terrain without the ducks seeing me, looking for dry spots to step on. I opened the gate fast, closed it behind me, ran in, chunked the pail of leftover food and ran back out of the pen before they stuck me in the butt with their bills. They laughed, quacked and cackled like hens laying eggs but I made it out. Beat you, dummies! Try again tomorrow.

I also learned how to weave lauhala hats from the leaves of the hala tree. A Polynesian woman (mother of a friend) sat with me under the shade of our house and patiently showed me how to weave. My first attempt at Arts and Crafts. Never got to take the next step up to weaving mats, etc.

Around age 12, my wondering came back to me. I wondered what was in all of those books in the elementary school library and why no one read them. When the school closed for the summer break, I asked the Principal for permission to use the library. Being my dad, he said to have at it. I read every book in there, absorbed all that my brain could handle. It actually came in handy 5 years later. Our high school senior year, Social Studies Teacher, stopped every day for 15 minutes to ask trivia questions out of a book that he had. I was able to raise my hand, answer the questions and appear smart.

B.   COFFEE HARVEST

The 1940's and 1950's were difficult economic years for the residents of Kona, Hawaii. Almost everyone depended on the growth and sale of Kona coffee. Dad bought 7-8 acres of abandoned coffee trees to help supplement his income. It seemed like we worked forever to bring the trees back into production. He also started a local Credit Union which aided the struggling coffee farmers.

Coffee harvesting season started in September and lasted until Thanksgiving. Like most of my friends and classmates, our proceeds went into buying food and supplies.

A typical harvest day started at 4am. We wore a light jacket to ward off the early morning chill, reluctantly jumped into the back of a WW II open jeep for a 30 minute ride to our plot of land. Sister rode shotgun, I huddled in the back trying to avoid the breeze. When we got there, we sat around waiting for first light. Oh wow! It's light already, I just dozed off. Time to get started.

Each one of us had a personal, rickety, wooden 5 ft. ladder and a lauhala woven basket with a waist strap that fitted us. Time to attack the trees. Reach up through the spider webs and wet leaves to grab the top of the branch and slide your hand down it plucking out all the red and reddish-yellow berries, letting them drop into your basket. You move your fingers as if playing the piano. Get off my hand you furry creature, I'll squash you later. Reposition the ladder on the rocky, sloping ground to pick around the back of the tree. Isn't this fun? The sun rises, steam rises, it is hotter. Off comes the jacket, and anything else. Time to sweat a lot.

For the newcomers, picking one berry at a time simulates sitting at Daytona Raceway gunning your engine but going—nowhere waiting for the white flag. Dad picked 400 lbs. per day, I picked 300, sister Elaine 250-300 and any newcomer 50. I'll tell you a secret, Elaine picked a lot of borderline yellowish-green berries also. She is still picking coffee but as an entrepreneur. A retired Kindergarten School Teacher, she also dries and sells opelu (Pacific Mackerel Scad). Husband George catches the opelu and delivers the dried fish to regular customers. Their orders are in high demand and backlogged. They now fly up to Reno to golf and hit the slots. Also, they go to Vegas twice a year. I struggle all year to scrape up enough money to go to Vegas once a year. May be I should have picked some yellowish-green berries also.

We took an hour lunch break, then wearily dragged ourselves back to work as the 4am wake-up got to us. Except for dad, he jumps up and heads back out to hit it again—Attack the trees, ripple the berries! If he could whistle, he would whistle a happy tune. We start again….slowly. Someone turns on the radio, a cheerful voice describes how wonderful and beautiful it is today on Waikiki Beach. I am torn between relaxing to the music or strangling the D.J.

It finally starts to darken around 6pm. Dad sews the 100 lb. burlap bags full of coffee beans closed and we load up around 1,000 lbs. of coffee berries and deliver them. Heading for home, looking forward to another 4am wake-up tomorrow, another long, dreary day. This goes on for 3 months, 7 days a week.

No surfing, sun tanning on sandy beaches or sleeping in. Our school break deliberately matched the harvest season, September to Thanksgiving. We were out of sync. with all the other school systems in Hawaii.

Tourists dream of coming to Hawaii, we dream of getting off the island and seeing the world.

CHAPTER THREE

Memories of Spectacular Events

Between the ages of 8 to 17, I experienced amazing occurrences. Molten rock acting like colored water, the earth trembling like a frightened child watching Freddy Krueger, the damage done by a huge wave of water reaching ½ mile inland. It all happened on the island I lived on—The Big Island of Hawaii.

A. TSUNAMI

On April 1, 1946, a massive 100 foot high tsunami created by an earthquake in the Aleutian Islands, measuring 8.6 on the Richter Scale started racing toward Hawaii. 2370 miles and 4.9 hours later, it reached the northeastern coast of the Big Island at 7am. A 100 foot high wall of water spreading out to 100 miles wide and dropping to 2 foot high, traveling at approximately 490 mph. Upon reaching shallower water it lost some speed, changed back to 23-30 feet high and reached Hawaii.

The tsunami destroyed downtown Hilo with waves approximately 27 feet high. The wave receded back out to sea sucking everything loose out with it. The bay was left empty of water. Children walking out on the bare sand to gather live fish and shells were killed by the returning waves. A total of 159 deaths occurred and 153 people seriously injured. The waves pounded Hilo and Laupahoehoe. 96 deaths in Hilo and 24 in Laupahoehoe.

Hard to believe, hard to envision what happened on April Fool's Day, 1946.

Imagine waking up on April Fool's Day at 7am and being told to run for your life, as far inland as possible. Oh c'mon. I won't fall for that trick. Back to sleep.

Drop that cup of coffee, turn the stove off, grab your children and run. Don't look back, run for your lives!

It was a shocking surprise for everyone. No warning, no previous killer tsunami and of all days-- April Fool's Day at 7 in the morning.

After lunch on that day, dad loaded us into the car and drove to Hilo, on the opposite side of our island. We had no relatives or friends living there, he just wanted to see what happened. I was 8 years old, too young to relate to what I saw. All that I remember was seeing everything flattened. No standing houses, no buildings, just scattered rubble.

The most comprehensive, detailed study of the 1946 tsunami was done by FP Shepard, GA Macdonald and DC Cox, published in a bulletin of the Scripps Institute of Oceanography, March, 1950. It is an impressive document.

Tsunamis travel in 2 opposite directions from an oceanic earthquake. One toward the nearest landfall and the other out to sea. The tsunami that traveled toward landfall hit Scotch Cap, southwest tip of Unimak Island, largest of the Aleutian Islands, Alaska. It destroyed a lighthouse and crew sitting 98 feet above sea level. The wave height was estimated to be 115-135 feet. Since Unimak Island is sparsely populated. The destruction of the US Coast Guard lighthouse prevented any transmission of the danger to Hawaii.

We envision a tsunami as a giant wave of water racing across the ocean, not true. In the open water, tsunamis measure 2-3 feet high, spread 50-100 miles wide, moving very fast.

The 1946 tsunami was 2 foot high, 100 miles wide, moving at approximately 484 miles per hour out to sea. The epicenter was 90 miles south of Unimak Island. Being only 2 foot high, it was not seen by ocean traffic.

Upon reaching shallow waters, tsunami's speed reduces, the height becomes higher and steeper. Tsunamis are actually a series of waves. Sometimes the first wave is the highest, sometimes the 3rd or 4th, or sometimes the last wave is highest.

There were previous tsunamis in Hawaii, but not as powerful as this one.

April,1868—10 ft. waves in Hilo, 8 ft. in Kealakekua
August, 1868—15 ft. in Hilo
August, 1872—4ft. waves in Hilo
May, 1877—12ft. waves in Hilo, 5 deaths in Waiakea District (Hilo)
August, 1901—4 ft. waves in Kailua
January, 1906—12 ft. waves in Hilo
February, 1923—20 ft. waves in Hilo (3rd wave)
March, 1933—10 waves in Kailua

Living next to the ocean is beautiful but sometimes quite hazardous. Natural occurrences can be devastating.

B.   EARTHQUAKES

Imagine walking outdoors, doing your usual routine and suddenly your legs buckle, you have no balance, can't stand up, can't see anything that is immobile to right yourself by looking at it. Everything is shaking! You stumble toward something familiar but get disoriented. Finally, you decide to get on your hands and knees and crawl toward a building to lean against something solid. Then your sense of reasoning kicks in. Since everything is shaking, including this building, what if it falls and crushes me? So you get on your belly and crawl away from it.

There is no place to go to, you start getting sick. You stop and roll over. Look at the sky, it is swaying too. Close your eyes and try not to think. If the earth opens up and swallows me, it will be sudden. If the building falls, I won't see it coming.

13 year olds have an active imagination but little knowledge. 77 year olds have acquired lots of knowledge but it doesn't help. We still have a scary imagination.

Finally, it stops, I'm alive! I will get to see another sunset, get my drivers permit, dream another dream. These series of heavy tremors on May 29, 1950 put me in a somber mood for a month. I kept wondering if the next time, maybe I won't be so lucky.

Earthquakes happen suddenly, last for a few minutes and stop. They sometimes come in a series of tremors, all very upsetting. Two days later, Mt. Mauna Loa erupted.

C. VOLCANOES

Hawaii has a spectacular event which it shares with only one other state—Alaska, live volcanoes.

Mt. Mauna Loa (13,677 feet high from sea level) erupted during the late night hours of June 1, 1950. The eruption was spectacular. A 12 mile long fissure in the southeast sloping top of the mountain opened to vent fountains of lava (red hot liquid rock) 300 feet into the air along the entire 12 mile length. The lava poured out in separate outbreaks along the 12 mile fissure to form 7 separate rivers of liquid lava (magma) flowing down the mountain. 5 flows headed toward the southern end of Kona, not too far away from where we lived. The first flow was very fluid and fast. It moved rapidly downslope 12 miles to the sea in only 3 hours. It was relentless, covering everything in its path. The lava cooled quickly on the surface leaving a hardened look. You could try walking on it if you dared. Under the hardened surface, the lava still flowed, a river of red hot rock.

Dad woke us up in the middle of the night to drive out to see the lava flow. Wrapped in blankets, armed with several thermos full of hot coffee, we dozed in the back of the car until he could drive no further. I did not know what adventure we were on, what we were about to see. We walked on the paved road about half a mile to where the lava flow covered the road. As we came closer, the strong smell of sulfur dioxide was in the air and we could feel the heat from the lava flow.

There were small pockets of visible, reddish yellow areas with steam rising from them along the side of the road as we approached the flow.

No way am I going to touch that rock or even try to walk on it.

The next day, I walked to a little grocery store up the street where I encountered a friend and his dad. They owned a fishing boat and were on their way to view the eruption from the sea. They had room for one more passenger—me. We headed out to sea, followed the coastline until we came to the third and most active flow that reached the ocean.

There it was, a river of red and yellow liquid rock. You could see the full picture—where it started on the mountain top to where it entered the ocean, approximately 1 mile from where we floated. The water was warm, dead fish floated around us. The view was unbelievable.

Being in the right place at the right time allowed me to see this special view of Mt. Mauna Loa's lava flow in its entirety. When

I got home, it took me a week to pacify my mother's concern for her disappearing son. She had had severe rheumatoid arthritis and went to bed after teaching school all day. I tried to ask her but she was sleeping and I didn't want to wake her. I would be with a responsible family and I didn't realize that we would be gone until 10pm. Wrong decision for a 13 year old to make.

We didn't own cameras but this beautiful image of the lava flow remains imbedded in my memory and I imagine, in the rest of the viewers on the boat. Heavy overcast skies prevented airplanes from flying over the area, you had to approach it from a boat to see this special view.

The island of Hawaii has another very active volcano, Kilauea. It's mountain top was levelled by a violent explosion in the past leaving a caldera (volcanic crater), 3 miles long, 2miles wide and approximately 270 feet deep. The rim height of the caldera is 4200 feet above sea level.

Although very active in the past, Kilauea was inactive from 1934 to 1952. We could drive into the mountain top to a parking lot by the Hawaiian Volcano Observatory and look into Halemaumau Crater—a firepit in the center of the caldera, approximately ½ mile round and 800 feet deep. It is a huge hole in the ground with a gray volcanic bottom.

Halemaumau Crater is the home of Pele, Hawaiian Goddess of fire, lightning, wind and volcanoes. Everything looks quiet, peaceful and non-threatening. SSSH! Don't wake her up, she's sleeping. Even if you don't believe in Hawaiian mythology, it doesn't hurt to be extra careful. Halemaumau has not erupted since 1934.

In 1952, she woke up. Kilauea erupted with a spectacular violence. On the night of June 27, a long fissure opened on the Halemaumau crater floor. For a half mile, fountains of lava shot out from 50 to 130 high with an additional fountain on the southwest edge shooting 800 feet high, topping the crater rim. The lava pouring out filled the crater floor.

At 4am the next day, the new lava was 50 feet deep with waves rolling across the top of it, splashing 10 feet up the crater wall.

The eruption continued until November 10, 1952. It slowly diminished in strength and volume. The new lava filled Halemaumau Crater 310 feet in depth, reducing it from 770 to 460 feet deep.

Dad has a way of knowing about these happenings. He never listens to the radio, we had no TV in 1952 but somehow, he knew. Early in the morning of June 28, he woke us and asked if we would like to see it. Sure, why not. So we again bundled in blankets and made the car trip halfway around the island. Got there about an hour before sunrise and got to see the eruption in darkness. It was wild and scary. There were perhaps 20 to 30 people walking along the crater edge looking down into the fire pit. In places, there was some protective fencing but for the most part, you walked out to the crater edge at your own risk. The image of the edge crumbling and falling into the pit some 700 feet down was always on my mind. I watched where everyone stepped and stepped exactly into that step while looking away from the crater to locate a spot that I could jump to in case the edge that I was stepping on did crumble away. It was scary but I did manage to look down into the red and yellow spectacle down below. We stayed until sunrise then drank our coffee, munched on some leftover munju (Japanese confection filled with red bean curd paste) then drove home.

My sister was not as chicken as I was. She strolled up to the edge, walked along it looking down into the fire pit and then nonchalantly walked back to the car. That morning, she definitely had more courage than I did. Later in life, she applied that "Go big or Go home" attitude to the slot machines in Vegas. I just put in a few coins and hope for the best.

Growing up in north Kona, we lived on the slope of Mt. Hualalai, 8,271 feet high. Never snow covered, always there behind us, protecting us. I've always considered it to be a safe, dormant mountain. To my surprise, while doing research for this book, I discovered that it really is an active volcano. It last erupted in 1801. Scientist believe that it will erupt again within the next 100 years. A lava flow to the western flank will cover Holualoa and Kailua within hours. More than half of the Kona coffee crop grows in north Kona. Wow! What an unwelcome surprise.

D. PELE

According to Hawaiian mythology, Pele controls all of the volcanoes on the Big Island. She wanders over her domain as a tall, beautiful young woman or as a very ugly and frail woman. She is accompanied by a white dog and frequently tests people. As an old beggar woman, she asks them if they have any food or water to spare. If you share with her, she spares you. If you don't, you are punished by having your home and property destroyed. She puts a curse on anyone disturbing or stealing from her domain.

I am cautiously respectful of anything having to do with Pele. For many years, I thought that the bright red Lehua blossoms belonged to Pele. I tried not to look at them, no touching or taking. I finally learned that the Lehua blossoms represented a woman and the Ohia tree represented an ancient Hawaiian warrior. Pele asked the young warrior to marry her but he told her that he was in love with a young girl named Lehua. Before he answered Pele, he made her promise not to destroy him or his property. She agreed. When he told her about Lehua, she became furious and turned him into a twisted tree. Lehua was heartbroken and asked the Hawaiian gods for help. They turned Lehua into a beautiful flower on the Ohia tree so that the two lovers would be forever together. Every time that someone picks a Lehua blossom, they are separating the two lovers and that day, it will rain their tears. A sad but beautiful legend.

CHAPTER FOUR

Start of a Life Long Journey

Finally, high school was over. Cap and gown ceremonies with speeches by classmates Donald and Carol. Thank goodness, I ended up third and no speaking obligations. I'm not a talker, hopefully a good writer but definitely not a talker. Think I had a B in trigonometry in the 9th grade and B's in chemistry and physics later. Did well in everything else, typed like a fiend in typing class and loved geometry, even solid geometry. I love to look at shapes.

A.   ON TOP OF THE WORLD

A week after graduation, I was invited by Cousin Jeannette and 11 others to join them on a great adventure. We all piled into 3 WW II open jeeps and headed out to climb Mt. Mauna Kea, 13,796 feet high, tallest mountain in the Hawaiian Island Chain. We started around 4am, drove almost due north for 40 miles to reach the Saddle Road between the two tall mountains (Mauna Loa and Mauna Kea) then another 20 or so miles to the start of the hiking trail, approximately at the 8,000 foot level. Got there at sunrise and started climbing the remaining 5,000+ feet. It was all cinder, gravel and lava rocks. You took 2 steps up and slid one step down. Took us 4 hours of climbing and sliding to reach the summit. Then, there was nothing above you but blue sky. Sun shining brightly, warm and exciting. On top of the world with our shirts off getting a suntan.

It was an unbelievable feeling to be able to look down on everything. We absorbed the feeling of being "King of the World" for 30 minutes, then we headed down. Took us only 2 hours to slip and slide down the mountainside to our jeeps. I will always remember this experience. It was a spontaneous, one-of-a-kind, special adventure.

B.   COLLEGE LIFE

5 years of college started out with great expectations. Accepted into the University of Hawaii's difficult School of Engineering, I had high hopes of doing well. Dad bought for me a state of the art bamboo slide rule. It served me well as I scrambled to study for 18 hours of credits per semester plus 1 additional summer session for half a day for surveying classes (outdoor work doing actual surveying). We were in school 8-5 Mon to fri and 8-12 on Saturday. While other students played in the afternoons and Saturday, we were in classes.

Social activities for engineering students were almost non-existent.

After 2 years of mandatory ROTC (Reserve Officers Training Course), we were offered a small allowance every month to continue on for 2 years of Advanced ROTC. I accepted and became a Squadron Commander, then a Lieutenant Colonel in charge of 3 squadrons of troops. I yelled......Right Turn, Hut! They all turned right...... Group Halt! They all stopped. I was a Group Commander in charge of approximately 100 men.

Great! Better than cold beer on a hot day, no side effects. It also put me into a unique fraternity, The Arnold Air Society, with our own clubhouse. It was some place to go and relax during the lunch hours.

We marched in the May Day Parade for several miles from Honolulu to Waikiki Beach. Past a Reviewing Stand, they all stood, we saluted. We were foot sore and weary for days afterward.

For most of the 5 years of college, I lived with my uncle Joseph. He went to work on Eniwetok Atoll building wooden structures. They were preparing to measure the effects of hydrogen bomb testing. He would not talk about his work, just that it was very hot on the atoll.

At that time, no-one knew about the hydrogen bomb and its explosive power, more than 20 times stronger than that of the atomic bomb dropped on Japan. It was our secret weapon against our largest enemy, Russia. Little did I know that I would be flying on B-52 bombers on airborne alert just a few years later. We carried nuclear bombs, ready to drop them on Russian targets. We flew up to the Arctic Circle, then over to Greenland and back in to the US and home. We were replaced by other bombers, in the air covering critical targets. We also had bombers ready to launch upon 10 minutes notice while we lived in underground alert facilities sitting ground alert. About 1/3 of our bomber fleet sat or flew on airborne alert around the clock. We were re-fueled mid-air by tankers also sitting on alert. Fighters carrying a smaller nuclear payload also sat on alert in South Korea, Japan and Okinawa.

Another cap and gown ceremony. This time outdoors at night in the University of Hawaii Amphitheater. I Received my B.S. in Civil Engineering and a commission as an officer in the United States Air Force.

C. PREPARING TO LEAVE HOME

Now, a long wait for my Air Force orders to arrive in the mail. Finally! Report to Hickam AFB, Honolulu. Check in, pick up a clothing allowance and shopping list to buy uniforms and accessories at the base clothing sales store and get assigned a seat on a commercial flight from Honolulu International Airport to San Francisco, and another flight from San Francisco to San Antonio, Texas. Attend one week of Officer Orientation in class 60-16 at Lackland AFB, San Antonio and then on to James Connally AFB, Waco, Texas for a year of Basic Navigator School. I did not qualify for pilot training, needed eyesight of 20-20. My eyesight was 20-25 but I did qualify for navigator training.

My aunt Hilda starched and pressed my khaki uniform to a sharp edge, cousin Beatrice shined my black shoes to a mirror finish and uncle Joseph drove me to the entrance gate at Hickam AFB. I showed my papers, got directions to where to report in and also receive further instructions. I received my first salute as a new, bright eyed and bushy tailed 2nd lieutenant. Wow! I can get used to that. Reported in and got scheduled on a commercial flight to San Francisco and another from San Francisco to San Antonio.

They assigned me to a middle seat between two business women. It was a pleasant flight for 8 hours on a Pan American propeller driven airplane. The lady sitting in the window seat next to me swapped seats so that I would get my first view of the Golden Gate Bridge and San Francisco. If everyone was that thoughtful and kind, this would be a wonderful journey. Mainland 49 states, here I come!

CHAPTER FIVE

The Journey Begins

I became very excited as we got closer to San Francisco Bay. Then, there it was, a bright orange bridge in startling contrast with the dark blue skies and bluish/ green ocean. Wait a minute, wasn't it supposed to be golden? Welcome to the land of golden opportunities?

Everyone seated around me was expecting my chagrined look and they all explained that unlike the Statue of Liberty in New York, the Golden Gate Bridge gets its name from the Golden Gate Strait which it crosses.

It was a wonderful sight welcoming me to the upper 49 states (mainland).

My Uncle James met me at the airport and we drove back into San Francisco. I spent 2 days visiting my Uncle and Aunt Lily then back in the air again. Flew across half the country to San Antonio, Texas for a week of Officer Orientation School at Lackland, AFB. Got there 2 days early so I spent the time walking around the downtown area.

Walked to the Alamo where 240 Texians fought 3,100 Mexicans in a battle to the death. The Texians were considered pirates by Santa Anna, he raised the red flag: No mercy! No quarters! James Bowie, William Travis, Davy Crockett died here in a valiant effort to delay Mexican president, Santa Anna's roll north to secure all of Texas for Mexico.

A. THE ALAMO

I respect the valiant efforts of the 240+ Texians but with 13 to 1 odds against them, why didn't they retreat to a better position with more forces? And Santa Anna, with an army of 3100 men, why didn't he attack immediately and occupy the entire region?

Like many other visitors with only a passing knowledge of the battle of the Alamo, I thought that the Texians were comprised entirely of white settlers who had migrated to the Texas frontier. They made their stand in a well- fortified frontier fort. When I actually saw the Alamo, it was a small Spanish mission with walls partly destroyed by Mexican cannon fire. Historians say that there were approximately 182 to 257 defenders of the Alamo. Mexican President Santa Anna had approximately 3,100 in San Antonio de Bexar San Antonio) when the siege began. 600 were killed in the battle. The initial defenders consisted of 13 native born Texians defending their homeland plus 2 Jews and 2 blacks. The rest of the defenders were 41 Europeans and Americans from other states. James Bowie arrived with 30 men, William B. Travis with 30 men and a small group of volunteers arrived with Tennessee Congressman Davy Crockett.

I live in Texas and since I don't want to get killed by irate Texans, I will depart from the historians and only give you the generalized version of the battles.

The battles started on February 23, 1836 and ended 13 days later on March 6. For the first 12 days, there were only minor skirmishes with very little casualties. Both sides resorted to artillery fire.

On March 5, prior to the Mexican assault, Colonel Travis assembled all the men to inform them of the odds against them and gave them a choice. Escape now or stay and die for the cause. Anyone who wished to escape should say so and step out of ranks. No one chickened out.

Early in the morning of March 6, Santa Anna attacked. On the third assault, the Mexicans went over the 9-12 foot walls and killed all the Texian soldiers in the interior buildings. The battle was over by 6:30 am. Non-combatants, women and children were spared. And so ended the Battle of the Alamo, all defenders killed.

On March 2, 1836, Sam Houston was appointed sole commander of all Texian troops by the newly formed "Republic of Texas ". Starting with an army of 400 men, he gathered additional men who were incensed, actually pissed by the defeat at the Alamo. He retreated eastward, Santa

Anna followed. In a surprise move, the Texian army turned around and attacked. The Texians attacked with the battle cry of "Remember the Alamo ". The battle of San Jacinto was over in 18 minutes, the Mexican army soundly beaten and Santa Anna captured the next day.

Plaques on the walls of the ruins gave me some knowledge of what had happened, where Davy Crockett, Sam Bowie and Colonel Travis fought and died. In 1959, the Alamo looked as if it was abandoned yesterday, after the battle.

OK, I'm in Texas, where are all the cowboys riding their horses? Open ranges with herds of cattle? Where is the Marlboro Man who inspired me to take up smoking? Maybe roll a few of my own using a Bull Durham pouch. It was a crazy way to look cool, a nice way to cut 10 years off your life and die young.

Oil happened—Black gold. Large cities, 4 lane highways, civilization had reached Texas.

B. NAVIGATOR SCHOOL

Started Basic Navigator School at James Connally AFB, Waco, Texas during the first week of October, 1959. There were 21 students in my class. Around half of the class was married and lived off-base, the rest of us lived on-base in a BOQ dorm with individual rooms. We all got along pretty well and supported each other.

We went to classes during the day with some time also spent on physical training. During the 11 months of school, we flew on 37 training missions in T-39's specially outfitted as flying classrooms. They had 14 student radar and navigation tables and 4 astrodome bubbles for sextant readings.

During the day, we studied map reading, dead reckoning, the weather, radio signals, radar, low level flying, over water navigation, night triangulation with the stars, day techniques using a sextant, loran, etc. Loran is now obsolete, replaced by GPS. Some GPS systems utilize an annoying female voice which keeps reminding you that you screwed up.

We flew the T-39 flights from February to September, 1960. All of the students were not used to flying and struggled to complete their training while half-air sick. My biggest problem was in identifying stars to fix on. I had a difficult time seeing the different constellations.

We had several night classes out in the middle of the grassy area between buildings, away from lights. We lay on our backs looking up at the starry Texas sky. We looked for the different Constellations, rotated our current Air Almanac Star Chart to match what we saw. Big Dipper and Little Dippers, Belt of Orion, Leo, Virgo, etc. It was very peaceful and quiet until my classmates started telling old jokes. Some were funny, others got booed. Here are some samples:

What does a blonde say when you blow in her ear?
Answer: Thanks for the refill". Boo !

Why does a refrigerator hum?
Answer: "Because it doesn't know the words ". Boo!

I was standing in an auto parts store one day and overheard a well -built woman asking for a seven-ten cap. She had lost hers. "It has always been on the engine of my Chevy—around 3 inches in diameter and now it is missing ". She drew a picture of it (710), the manager went to get her an oil cap. Turn this page around and laugh.

We learned about military and flying language. How to talk in Zulu time, speak in understandable alphabets—Alpha, Beta, Charlie, etc. How to say Roger—Sir! Army sucks, Navy sucks, Air Force flies. Helmets are not to be used for throwing up in. Pay particular attention to buckling on a parachute and remembering where the location of both rip cords are. We are not Paratroopers, we don't have the luxury of hooking up to an overhead line and yelling "Geronimo". You could substitute :"Who in the hell pushed me!"

We learned about weather facts like Coriolis Force, red skies at night-sailor's delight, red skies in the morning-sailors take warning. High pressure systems rotate clockwise, low pressure systems counter clockwise, etc.

The rest of the bachelors included me in many of their weekend activities. We watched Baylor University play basketball, drove down past the oil refineries in Houston to Galveston to lie on the beach and watch the sea gulls and the girls. We drove up to Dallas to eat Chinese food.

Most of us had to scramble to make it through the month with our 2nd Lieutenant's pay. Without our flight pay, we would be starving and walking. Eating in the Officer's Club was a rare treat for me.

One weekend, three of my college ROTC classmates surprised me. They drove up from pilot training school to see me and invite me to join them on a drive down to visit Mexico. We drove down to Laredo, Texas, stayed in a motel called Papagaios, with a picture of a parrot on its sign located on the US side of the border, then walked over into Nuevo Laredo. We walked around seeing all the shops and ended with having a few beers in a Mexican bar. We talked and spent time with some senoritas, enjoyed the atmosphere. It was fun. A new experience for me in many ways. Got back to Waco refreshed and ready to finish out my training.

I flew on my last flight on September 7, 1960, graduated and received my wings. I became a real Air Force flyer! Next assignment: Bombardier School at Mather AFB, Sacramento, California. 7 paid travel days to get there plus another free day if I checked in before midnight.

CHAPTER SIX

Go West, Young Man

Wow! 7 full days to visit some of this great country. I headed north, out of Waco, Texas with a bag full of groceries and a small ice chest with bottled water and cokes. 2 loaves of bread, Vienna sausages, devil's mix, etc. I don't remember the names of the small cans, just that they tasted yuck! I didn't think about peanut butter. Also, a valuable thermos full of hot coffee. In 1960, there were no 24 hour convenience stores with hot coffee, food, snacks and gas. Gas stations opened around 6am and closed at 8pm.

The thrill of being out of the classroom and free for 8 days to travel, head out in any direction was overwhelming! Love it!

A. DODGE CITY

Heading north, destination Dodge City, Kansas. It is described as a wicked little town. Entertainment, history, excitement, old west atmosphere. 600 miles of hard driving, hopefully only 10-11 hours away.

Dodge City was a frontier cow town, the most wicked town in the old west. Advertised as all that is wild, reckless and violent. "Hell on the Prairie". Home to Wyatt Earp, Doc Holliday, Big Nose Kate, Clay Allison.

Started in 1872 to service soldiers from nearby Fort Dodge, Dodge City boomed in 1876 with the arrival of the railroad. The Atkinson, Topeka & Santa Fe Railroad brought in provisions, grain and flour.

Buffalo hides and meat were shipped out. Texas longhorn cattle were driven north along the Chisolm Trail to Dodge City.

Kansas established a quarantine against splenic fever just east of Dodge City. Approximately 1.5 million buffalo hides were shipped from Dodge City from 1872 to 1878. From 1875 to 1885, over 5 million head of cattle arrived in Dodge City for shipment. Dodge City boomed for 10 years as a famous frontier settlement of the old west with gun fighters, saloons, gambling halls, brothels.

In 1885, Kansas moved the quarantine line across all of Kansas. Dodge City became a sleepy little town.

I arrived in Dodge City, Kansas in the afternoon. Walked around the main street, looked at window displays, could not find an old saloon to have a sarsaparilla drink, like in the old days. Kept on walking to Boot Hill Cemetery, so named because all the gunfighters died with their boots on and not in a safe bed. I walked around the cemetery looking for a recognizable name—found none. Very disappointing. Well, so much for Matt Dillon and the characters of "Gunsmoke", learned later that it was filmed on ranches in California plus some scenes in Utah, Arizona and South Dakota.

Remember the TV show "Gunsmoke"? Maybe you've seen old re-runs of it? It was a must see weekly western that ran for 20 years from 1955 to 1975. It was set in the frontier town of Dodge City.

Marshall Matt Dillon, Miss Kitty, Doc, Chester etc. Lots of villains, card sharks, land takers, rustlers. Action every week with the good guys winning. It had everything that could happen in a rough, wild west town. Cattle rustling, gunfights, brawls, land fraud, kidnappings. Well almost everything. No alien sightings, female hugging, butt grabbing, no sex.

The plot moves slowly but was compelling. It kept you wondering what would happen next before Marshall Matt Dillon finally stepped in to save his friends and Dodge City. He always did.

"Gunsmoke" became one of the most popular TV shows in the history of television. The first 6 years were half hour programs and the last 14 years, One hour shows once a week. The last 9 years were in color. It holds the record for the longest running drama on TV, 20 years.

"Bonanza" ran for only 14 years.

James Arness appeared as Matt Dillon in every one of the 635 episodes. Milburn Stone as Doc. And Amanda Blake as Miss Kitty appeared in 568 episodes. Burt Reynolds appeared as one of the deputies for 4 years.

No more attractions past Boot Hill, still daylight, I'm turning west and driving on.

B.   ROCKY MOUNTAINS

Reached Denver, Colorado around 10pm, decided to spend the night in a motel to rest for the next day's journey into the mountains.

I got up early the next morning, had my thermos filled with hot coffee, gassed up and headed up into the mountains. Time to cross The Great Divide and see what's on the other side. From the Pacific Ocean to the flat lands of Texas and now the mountains with cooler temperatures and trees, lots of trees. Yellow aspen, whole mountainsides of yellow aspen trees, all connected together underground. Also, beautiful stands of fir, pine and juniper trees along the drive to the top. Finally reached a 180 degree turn in the road. The craggy, bare ridge line must be up above me, just past all these trees. So I drove on keeping an eye out for a sign that said Fall River Pass, 11,796 elevation. Trees, lots of trees, but no bare craggy ridge line. No stopping place to look down and yell---Hello! I can see you sun tanning, nice body. Smile! You must remember, I was a young bachelor, then.

I drove on slowly, looking for any sign of the elevation. Finally, 12 miles from Estes Park, there's a sign---Continental Divide, elevation 10,758 feet. I must be on the other side of the ridge line so I turned around and drove to the 180 degree in the road and started back. Again, I reached the Continental Divide not seeing the ridge line. Being a civil Engineer, I should have known that the Continental Divide is actually a division of 2 huge drainage areas. One flowing westward to the Pacific Ocean and the other flowing eastward toward the Atlantic Ocean and Gulf of Mexico. It was not a craggy ridge line. I had crossed the highest point and not known it.

I had expected to see a barren ridge top but all I could see was trees and more trees. Unlike the top of Mt. Mauna Kea, you could not look down and see civilization far, far below you. I finally gave up and drove down.

When you think about the Rocky Mountains, you envision just that—rocky mountains. You pull into a lookout, stand on an outcrop of boulders, look west and yell.......Hello!! How far to the Pacific and white beaches? Turn the other way and see amber waves of grain, faces carved on a mountainside, the Mighty Mississippi River.

C. YELLOWSTONE NATIONAL PARK

I drove down from the mountains to Loveland, then straight north to Cheyenne, Wyoming. It is located in the high plains, southeastern corner of Wyoming. I gassed in Cheyenne, took a short break to grab a sandwich and refill my thermos, then, turned due west.

Driving through rugged country with grasslands and mountain ranges, I saw herds of elk in open ranges, moose by Jackson, Wyoming and the magnificent Grand Teton Range. The Grand Teton Mountain Range is one of the most beautiful scenic views in my memory. It compares equally with the Grand Canyon.

There are 9 significant peaks in this range, from Static Peak at 11,300 feet to Grand Teton Peak at 13, 770 feet. The mountain range is raw, rising steeply with no foothills. Bring your own tea bags, no manzanita leaves to pick here.

Going westward through the rangelands between the mountain ranges was a beautiful experience. I saw no-one. Wyoming is the least populated state in the U.S. The western two thirds of the state consist of mountain ranges while the eastern one thirds is a high elevation prairie called the High Plains. There are over 40 mountain peaks taller than 13,000 feet with the highest being Gannett Peak, 13,804 feet.

I drove around Jackson for a while but seeing no-one moving, I decided to stop wandering and head north to Yellowstone National Park for shelter in a lodge. You picture sitting around a roaring fire, drinking hot toddies and warming your feet. But, not today or tomorrow. The park is closing for the season on Sunday. They rented me a room to sleep in for 2 days. No maid service, no open restaurants, everything was closed. Drag out the stale bread, open a can of Vienna sausages and drink some tap water.

Lodging acquired, it is time to drive over to see the famous "Old Faithful". There it is! With a roar, a geyser of boiling water shooting straight up. Wow, spectacular!

It stopped before I could reach the observation point, have to wait another 91 minutes for the next eruption. Really, is it that reliable? I'll settle for a plus or minus 15 minutes. I walked around, read all the signs and waited. Here it comes! Old Faithful, right on schedule, amazing!

Steamboat Geyser is the tallest geyser in Yellowstone Park. It has been quiet since 1911.

2 hours left before sunset, time enough to drive around and see other sights. I walked on a boardwalk to see the beautiful colors of Grand Prismatic Spring, also to see the Bubbling Paint Pots. It is hard to believe that the bubbling mud is boiling hot. The smell of sulfur dioxide is everywhere. Some people call it smelling rotten eggs. It reminds me of standing next to a fresh lava flow in Kona, same smell. Back to the lodge for a nights rest.

Up early the next morning, no cars, no tourist around. No coffee! As I wandered around looking for any place open for coffee, a kind worker shared her thermos of coffee with me before continuing her work.

I visited Old Faithful again before exploring other parts of the park. Around midday, I had to stop. Traffic was backed up around a curve. We finally moved slowly up to the curve and witnessed a crazy sight. Two cars were parked in the middle of the road with families feeding sandwiches to 3 black bears. One bear climbed onto the hood of the first car to look in for more food while the other two bears ambled over to the second car looking for a hand out. They stood on their hind legs and looked into the door windows. The families didn't realize what a dangerous situation they had put themselves into by feeding the bears. They ran out of sandwiches and rolled up their windows. Both bears climbed onto the hood of their car. You don't just pat them on the head or rump and say, that's all I have, sorry. You do that to dogs or maybe partners if you're brave, but not to bears. People in the cars behind them threw boxes of food onto the side of the road to distract the bears. We were then able to drive slowly around the bears while they opened the lunch boxes and devour the food. I visited the bubbling mud pots once more, smell more sulfur dioxide, watched Old Faithful erupt on time once again. I then headed back to the lodge to get to bed early. They were closing the park gates the next day and I had to roll out early.

D. WHERE THE BUFFALO ROAM

Got up at 4am, drove out heading due east into the rising sun. 500 miles to Custer City, South Dakota for lunch. Look, there's a café with a large sign advertising buffalo burgers. I must stop and eat one. It was a treat to get off the road, rest and eat something new and exotic. The burger was sweet and different.

Between Yellowstone and Custer City, I didn't see a single buffalo, where have they all gone? I asked the waitress and she gave me directions to follow. 5 miles up ahead, turn right onto a country road and when you see an open gate with a cattle grate, drive in. Away I went, followed her instructions drove across the cattle grate and onto a dirt road leading down the center of a wide open pasture. Wow! I see them, a herd of 25-40 buffalo.

I slowly approached the herd, they ignored me. Drove through the middle of them and turned around, they finally noticed me. I drove a little faster, they started to amble along on either side of me. Wow! Up close and personal. They ran alongside of me as I drove toward the gate. It finally dawned on me that "what if one of them veered over, bumping into the car? I would be stranded in the middle of an open pasture, no-one around, at least a ten mile walk out to civilization." I speeded up, the buffalo started to gallop. We raced for a while as my heart started to beat faster. The open gate in sight, the buffalo gave up the race and I drove across the cattle grate to safety. Whatever possessed me to drive among those huge buffalo? It was a wild experience that will stay with me forever. Scared the hell out of me but I loved it.

Just 17 miles to Mt. Rushmore to see an amazing tribute to man's ability to overcome a near impossible task—carve a 60 foot high face, 4 faces to be exact, on a solid granite mountainside. Started in 1927, it was completed in 1939. Using dynamite, Gutzon Borglum and son Lincoln carved the faces of Washington, Lincoln, Jefferson and Theodore Roosevelt on Mt. Rushmore.

Driving into a graveled lookout, I looked up and there it was— perfect likenesses of 4 presidents carved into the side of the mountain. Who can imagine that someone could possibly do that? Beautiful, perfect images!

I must bring my future descendants to see this and also definitely a camera.

Westward Ho, young man! Follow the setting sun to Butte, Montana.

E.   ON THE ROAD AGAIN

Then, on to see Glacier National Park,300 miles north of Butte. Walk up to a glacier and touch the ice formed 100,000 years ago. The glaciers are slowly disappearing but maybe I can experience seeing them before they melt.

After a hard 6 hour drive to Cody, Wyoming, I stopped at the statue of Buffalo Bill Cody to decide whether to press on and drive the 260 miles to Butte Montana, or stay at a motel and rest. Finally, compromise was my decision. Stop at a café, eat a decent sandwich, fill my thermos with hot coffee and wait for the sun to go down before pressing on. After all, it was early evening and I wasn't very tired. One significant fact never entered my mind—I still had to cross over the Rocky Mountains at night on a narrow two lane road.

With a full tank of gas, thermos of hot coffee, my belly filled, I started out on the scenic 260 miles to Butte, Montana. 260 miles at a moderate 60 miles per hour should take me 4 ½ hours to reach Butte around midnight, find a motel and rest.

The road turned into a narrow 2 lane mountain road. Sheer drop off on your right with no barrier of any kind to keep you from sliding off. Look ma, I'm flying! Crash! Splat, blood! Scenic route my Okole! 30 miles per hour bent over, hugging the steering wheel, peering at the barely visible center line, my butt hurts from squeezing it so tightly for hours. Try squeezing your butt cheeks together and holding it. It's not fun. I'm afraid to look to the right at the steep drop off. My neck and shoulder muscles ache from being so tense. My fingers are cramping and locked from gripping the steering wheel so long.

Finally, Butte, Montana in sight. Yeah! At 2am it's too late to find a motel open and too cold to sleep in the car. 5,000 feet high, in a hollowed out basin straddling the Continental Divide, Butte is way too high in elevation and cold to hang around at night for the next 5 hours.

Wait a minute, this could be my lucky day. I see a truck stop still open. Gas up, fresh thermos of hot coffee, roll on. South to warmer temperatures. I have a lifetime left to come back and touch a glacier.

Rolling through Idaho at night. Sorry I can't see the beauty of this state. Gassed up early in the morning in Pocatello, kept on rolling south to Salt Lake City, Utah. This would have been a beautiful scenic drive during the daytime.

It ended up being a very short delay on a cold morning in Salt Lake City, Utah, trying to visit the Mormon Tabernacle. It is a huge wooden building. 150 feet wide and 250 feet long held together entirely by wooden pegs—dowels and wedges. The roof sits on sandstone pillars, no nails. Much to my disappointment, it was surrounded by a high wrought iron fence and a large sign saying: "No visitors, members only". Gate locked on a Sunday morning. Oh well, so much for that. I really wanted to see a building built entirely by using no nails and maybe hear the famous Mormon Tabernacle Choir. I saw a golden Gabriel blowing his horn sitting on a high, steep pinnacle.

I kept the motor running with the heater on while I checked the map for the location of the Bonneville Salt Flats. Since the city is named Salt Lake City, I was surprised to learn that it is actually 110 miles due west. I'm too tired and cold to make the 4 hour detour. Another time, another day.

Heading south out of town, destination Las Vegas. I finally stopped for an hour break at a nice roadside café for gas, food, supplies, hot coffee to fill my thermos and visit with some nice people.

Back on the road again heading southwest. The song from the TV show, "Rawhide" keeps ringing in my ear. "Rollin, Rollin, Rollin. Keep them dogies moving, Rawhide. Head em up, head em out, keep them dogies moving, --Rawhide"! A very young Clint Eastwood starred in this TV series. 425 miles, 6 hours to Las Vegas.

Driving southwest from Cedar City, Utah, to St. George, Utah, I began to see a reflection of light in the clouds above the horizon. Am I heading straight for a thunderstorm or a wildfire? It persisted and grew brighter as I kept driving. Only 3 hours from Las Vegas, hope they have a detour around it. A wide cloud of bright light in the sky up ahead.

"Rollin, Rollin, Rawhide! Thought the streams are swollen, keep them dogies rollin, Rawhide! Move em on, head em out, Rawhide!"

F. LAS VEGAS

As I get much closer, I start to realize that it is actually the lights of Las Vegas that I am seeing from so far away, reflected in the sky. Finally, I reached the source of the lights, downtown Las Vegas. It is broad daylight at 12 midnight. Wow!

Walking around, from casino to casino listening to the live music coming from the casino lounges was an awesome experience. The sound of coins clanking in the slot machines, people yelling when they won something and of course, everyone at the craps table yelling for their number to roll. Excitement all around you. It was contagious, you forgot your weariness and lack of sleep. I've run into a different world. You don't need to gamble, just walk around and absorb the atmosphere, enjoy.

I wandered over into Binion's Horseshoe Club and saw one million dollars on display. One million dollars in $10,000 bills, 100 of them.

I've never seen a $100 bill, a "c" note talked about in books. To see 100, $10,000 bills was unbelievable. I never even knew that they existed. I already love this town.

Someday, I will come back and hope for a lucky streak—win 1 million dollars and be set for life. The 4 silver dollars that I received in change after paying my dinner bill feels heavy in my pants pocket. How would you cart around 1 million silver dollars?

Just walking down Fremont Street was an experience. A huge neon cowboy down the street above the Pioneer Club waved his hand and said "Howdy Partner". Many, many, neon signs. Golden Nugget, Pioneer Club, The Mint Casino, Golden Gate, California Club, Binion's Horseshoe.

Some of the larger casinos were supposedly owned and run by the mob. If they didn't like you, you would stuffed in the trunk of a car, driven out into the desert, shot and left behind a sand dune. I kept reminding myself to keep my big mouth shut and try to be invisible. You don't want to make anyone mad, they could be part of the mob, even though they didn't wear wing shoes.

I finally ran out of steam and decided to sleep in the car until the sun came up.

Left Las Vegas around 8am heading for Reno. Goodbye lights. Goodbye sounds of coins clanking in the slot machines, goodbye excitement.

G. DONNER PASS

Just barely 2 hours driving northwest to Reno, a billboard came up saying: Turn left onto state route 373 to Bad Water Basin—292 feet below sea level, the lowest spot in the United States. This I must see and experience, it's only a 2 hour detour.

I drove into Furnace Creek, elevation 190 feet below sea level. Saw a group of buildings but no one around. No cars, no people. The entire place is abandoned. I got out of the car to stretch my legs....Boy, is it hot! Hotter than Waco, Texas where the temperature was around 99 degrees when I left. Read a sign saying: Furnace Creek, hottest temperature recorded in the U.S. 133 degrees, July 10, 1013.

I'm not driving any further into Death Valley. If my car overheats, I'm up a creek. It's at least a 50 mile walk back to the nearest town, maybe further. I was 15 miles from Bad Water Basin, that's close enough. Right now, I'm standing 190 feet below sea level.

Rolling out for Reno and then through Donner Pass. Winter weather at Donner Pass sometimes starts in late September and can become extreme. Wind gusts of over 100mph, average snowfall of 411 inches, record low temperature for California of -45 degrees recorded nearby in 1937, snow depths of over 20 feet. Briefed at the Newcomer's Briefing, Mather AFB, Sacramento, California that you were required to carry tire chains if you drove up to Donner Pass and into Reno from California in the winter. Sometimes, the snow flies up in the pass in September. Being the end of September, I decided that it would be a wise decision to get through the pass and into California as soon as possible. This is my 6th day on the road. I have 7 days to get to Mather AFB, any extra will count against my yearly leave.

Donner Pass is named after the Donner party of settlers who did not make it through the pass before the snows came. They camped at Truckee Lake to wait out the winter. Hardship, cannibalism and basic survival are all part of their story.

Crossing the wilderness is no picnic for experienced wilderness travelers but for ordinary families with just a dream of reaching the promised land—California, it could be extremely difficult. The Donner-Reed party was definitely not experienced in any way. George Donner 62 was a farmer and James Reed was a wealthy immigrant. They were joined by Donner's younger brother, Jacob. George's family totaled 6, Jacob's 8, and James's 6 plus 3 hired servants. They left Springfield, Illinois in early April, 1886 in 9 wagons heading for the start of the Oregon-California Trail at Independence, Missouri. Other families joined them along the way.

Arriving there in early May, they completed outfitting their wagons and joined a group of 50 wagons heading for Ft. Laramie, Wyoming and on to California. This was the last group of wagons on the Oregon-California Trail heading for Sutters Fort, California before snowstorms closed the pass through the Sierra Nevada Range. In 1886, 500 wagons had already preceded them.

Reaching Ft. Laramie, Donner and Reed heard of a short cut across the Wasatch Mountains and across the Great Salt Lake called Hastings "Cutoff". The wagon train left Ft. Laramie heading west, crossing the Rocky Mountains at South Pass, Wyoming then turned south toward Fort Bridger. Halfway there, the California Trail turned north and westward to go around the Great Salt Lake before heading southwest following the Humboldt River to the mountain pass leading into California.

A small group headed by George Donner left the wagon train and headed to Fort Bridger to join Hastings and follow him on the new shortcut.

Arriving at Fort Bridger, they found that Hastings had already left leading another group of 40 wagon trains. Jim Bridger, owner of the small trading post assured them that there was no rugged country to cross or hostile Indians. The route would shorten their journey by 350 miles. Water was easily available, they just had to cross a 40 mile dry lake bed.

He conveniently left out the part that no wagons had ever used this route.

Edwin Bryant, a journalist, had seen the first of the route and left letters with Jim Bridger telling future travelers to avoid the route at all cost. It would be too difficult for the Donner party. They never received the letters.

The Donner party decided to continue on, following Hastings onto the Hastings Cutoff.

It was an easy route to follow until they reached the Wasatch Mountains. Finding and following directions that Hastings had written on letters stuck to trees, the route became very steep. The men had to cut brush, trees and then move boulders to form a path for their wagons.

After leaving Fort Bridger on July 31, they finally reached the Great Salt Lake in early September.

Low on food and water, the Donner party still had to cross the Great Salt Lake. It was a barren plain covered with white salt. Looking innocent at first, the Great Salt Lake turned out to be a nightmare, freezing cold at night and very hot during the day. Adding to their misery, the daytime heat caused the moisture under the salt surface to rise up to the top and turn the surface into a gummy mess. The wagons sank into it, a lot of the oxen, cows and mules ran off to look for water. Finally crossing it in 6 days, they reached the original California Trail one month behind the original group. I would imagine that they wanted to kill Jim Bridger and Hastings for sending them into this nightmare. At least use every cuss words that they already knew or could dream up.

Without a lot of their animals and with damaged wagons, they had one more desert to cross. Finally crossing it while being harassed by Indians who stole their horses and cattle, they reached the Truckee River. It was lush country with grazing for their animals and water, a gift from heaven.

This was a perfect place to wait out the winter. Lots of water, grazing for their animals and game to hunt. They could easily reach California in the late spring.

But, they decided to press on, reach the promise land—California before the snows came. It was now October 20, but someone had advised them that the pass stayed open until the middle of November. At the start of their journey, they were also told that it snowed in the Sierras in September. Press on, get lucky seems to be the motto that they lived by.

The Donners were delayed by a broken axle and followed behind the rest of the group. The others made it up the vertical slope to Truckee Lake, 3 miles from the pass. It then began to snow but the families made their first attempt to cross the pass. They encountered 5-10 foot snow piles and no sign of the trail. Several more attempts were made to no avail. All 60 people in this group camped at Truckee Lake east of the pass in 2 separate cabins built by pioneers several years ago. The Donner families camped in tents next to Alder Creek 5 miles below them. It kept snowing and then turned into a storm that lasted 8 days until November 12.

The first group made 3-4 attempts to cross through the pass but failed. Snowed in, without food, they began to die. The living resorted to cannibalism, eating the ones that had died. OOH, WOW! Think about something else, that is sickening. YUCK! I really shouldn't judge them. If I were that desperate and hungry, I don't know what I would do.

A group of 17 men, women and children set out on snowshoes to cross the pass on December 21. Two turned back early, the rest continued on and became lost and confused, they were then snow blinded. Slowly, they died until only 7 remained to continue on. They reached a Miwok Indian camp. After several days of rest, William Eddy continued on with a Miwok guide to a ranch at the edge of the Sacramento Valley. A rescue party retrieved the remaining 6 survivors. It had taken them 33 days to cross the Sierras to safety in California.

In early February, an 11 man rescue party including William Eddy set out from Sacramento to rescue the Donner party. Eddy stopped along the way to wait, 3 others turned back, the remaining 7 made it across the pass to the group. They rescued 23 people, 18 children under 17 years old and 5 young adults. 33 people remained to be rescued.

In March and April, additional rescue parties retrieved the remaining survivors. They encountered blizzards, apathetic and exhausted families who refused to move. Some died and some came out later.

Of the 87 people in the Donner party who left Fort Bridger to take on the Hastings Cutoff, only 48 survived.

The Donner-Reed party was a victim of unusual circumstances but they brought most of it upon themselves by making poor decisions. They were not prepared to deal with the problems that came up.

The start of their journey was poorly planned. They did plan it to begin when the spring rains ended and grass for the animals was available but it got them into Independence, Missouri behind the approximately 500 wagons heading out for California in 1846. A wise decision was to follow them and try to catch them but they broke away from the 50 wagon train that they were in and follow the Hastings Cutoff without any prior knowledge of it. They ignored all warnings not to take it. A 350 mile shortcut route sounded so enticing, they couldn't resist.

Being ordinary families with no mountain skills, they were ill prepared to carve new wagon tracks across unknown territory. They had to move boulders, cut trees and brush to move their wagons through mountainous terrain, cross a salt covered flat plain that turned to mush in the daytime. Why didn't they attempt to cross it in the early morning hours when the surface had hardened a little? This was no normal crossing of a dirt plain. Upon reaching the Truckee River, why didn't they make camp for the winter? It was definitely too late to cross the Sierras by all advice given to them earlier. It sometimes snows in September in the Sierras or there's a driving blizzard in November or in March.

There was plenty of grass and water, comfortable surroundings for a perfect winter camp by the Truckee River.

What I learned from this long narrative is that you should truthfully assess your skills and abilities before taking on a new task. If you lack any knowledge or skills and abilities, by all means try to acquire them. Study, talk to experienced people, practice, prepare yourself. Do not dive in head first, surfs up! In the case of the Donner-Reed party, better preparation would have them with a smarter basis for making decisions. Just staying with the original wagon train and not taking the Hastings Shortcut would have gotten them safely into California. Speaking of snow flying in September, I better get through the pass and into Sacramento today. Thinking about the Donner-Reed party is really depressing. Cannibalism? Yeow! Sucking is ok but not eating flesh.

H.   SAN FRANCISCO

Rolled through Reno and up over the pass with my a/c running. It was hot in the mountains, no snow flying today. Drove down into Sacramento and Mather AFB on the evening of my 6th day on the road. Checked in the next morning and learned that Bombardier School did not start for another 6 days. I had 5 days left to complete my journey to finally run out of real estate driving west to the Pacific Ocean. San Francisco, city by the bay, here I come.

They assigned me to a room in a 3 bedroom duplex, in a quiet corner of the base housing. I will share it with 2 other Navigator School graduates from my class at Waco.

I unloaded all the few belongings that I possessed from my car and continued my quest to reach the Blue Pacific Ocean. I wanted to see the Pacific from ground level, drive the crookest street in the world, drive across the Golden Gate Bridge, see people hanging out of trolley cars and visit my Uncle James, Aunt Lily and family.

Finally, 7 days after leaving the middle of Texas, I drove across the Oakland Bay Bridge and into San Francisco. Journey completed, I could no longer drive westward.

I visited my aunt and uncle for 3 days, wandered around this beautiful city by the bay with its cold, humid climate. My first impressions of San Francisco were Wow! I need to buy a warm jacket, my warm blood cannot adjust to the cold and high humidity. The hills are really steep. They actually use parking brakes here. You need to use both feet at a stop sign, one on the brake to keep from rolling backward and the other to hit the gas when you moved forward. There were many unmarked 4 way intersections where you learned to play "chicken". First one into the intersections had the right of way. Look out for limousines, they don't stop. I must come back with a larger engine to play this game.

Cable cars clanked up and down the steep streets with people hanging out the sides. The cars were built with running boards so half of the riders could do this. Looks like fun. I would really like to come back and do that. I did get a chance to do it 4 years later on my honeymoon. We parked 3 blocks from Fisherman's Wharf, walked a block and got on a cable car. I grabbed a pole, leaned out the side, rode for 5 minutes down the hill, the car stopped. Everyone jumped off and walked away, including the grip man and conductor. It finally became obvious, we were at the Hyde-Beach turnaround, end of line. Must come back another day when we have more time.

We wandered over to Fisherman's Wharf. Couldn't help but look out into the bay and see Alcatraz Island only 1 ½ miles away. No prisoner ever swam the short distance and made it to land. 36 tried, 33 were accounted for and the other 3 believed to have drowned. Al Capone and Machine Gun Kelly had many friends but no one tried to "Spring" them.

My Uncle lived close to Golden Gate Park so I started each day by driving around the park looking at the beautiful blooming flowers. On the third day, the flowers were still blooming but a different color! It is really magical. I had to get out of the car and take a closer look. They were buried in pots buried in the dirt. Oh wow, sure fooled me. It is a very resourceful way to create such beauty.

CHAPTER SEVEN

Advanced Military Schools

I t was time to go back to Sacramento and Bombardier School.

A. BOMBARDIER SCHOOL

Funny how we were about to spend 9 months in Bombardier School learning how to drop a bomb in a square box using sophisticated, expensive equipment while a bird flying along at 100 feet high can hit a 2/12 by 5 foot rectangular auto windshield moving at 70 mph. Sometimes they start laughing and cackling too early and hit your back window.

It took us 4 months to learn what birds already knew, how to bomb accurately during daylight hours. We spent another 4 months learning what bats already knew. How to use radar and windage at night. But most important of all, how to get home.

School was fun, more technical than book learning along with 25 training missions in T-29 aircraft. We had a lot of weekends free. I would buy some cone sushi at a Japanese restaurant that I knew and head for San Francisco. A pleasant 1 ½ drive past a winery where you could get bombed drinking free samples, orange groves, past the pungent smell of onion fields wafting in the air and finally city living. I visited Uncle James, Aunt Lily and family once a month, maybe too often to be welcome.

We got a chance to look through a Norden Bombsight, a unique and very accurate piece of equipment used during World War II and the Korean War. It was made obsolete by nuclear warfare. Flashes from hydrogen bombs exploding around you, including those that you dropped, will blind you.

I finished Bombardier School in the hot summer of 1961. Received my first assignment as a flyer and not as a student. Homestead AFB, Homestead, Florida flying on a bomber crew as a navigator on the newest and last B-52H model bombers to be built. Oh, super! It is a great airplane and super location. Homestead AFB is just 20 miles south of Miami, Florida with white beaches and visiting bikini clad tourists. Women tourist from the west coast to the east coast. What a great adventure. First I had to attend B-52 flying school in Roswell, New Mexico at Walker AFB.

B.   B-52 FLIGHT SCHOOL

I trained on 12 B-52E flights at Walker AFB during the hot months, August and September 1961. Most of the other B-52 students were paired B-47 crew members moving up to B-52's. As a spare, I flew only with instructor crews, weekends off. I had lots of time between training flights and on weekends to wander around the area.

In the 6weeks that I spent at Roswell, not a single soul told me about an alien aircraft that crashed on a ranch outside of Roswell in 1947. The army collected everything that they could find, moved it to the airbase at Roswell, and then flew it out to Wright Patterson AFB in Ohio for storage. The army called it the remains of a weather balloon and closed the file on the Roswell incident.

Many original witnesses have now come forward with their version of the event. Roswell now uses signs of aliens for advertisement. I only recently learned of the crash from a lab technician, native of New Mexico as she performed an ultrasound on me prior to surgery in 2005, 44 years later.

Some of the witnesses describe 2 crash sites, one with dead alien figures lying on the ground. Many of the witnesses are highly credible individuals with professional backgrounds. One even took some material home to show to his son. It was very thin, easily crumpled into a ball.

When released, it sprang back to its original shape. Many theories associate the material with new technology but this happened in 1947. 14 years later, people were still keeping the crash a secret.

C. WINTER SURVIVAL SCHOOL

One more school left to attend, Winter Survival School at a camp somewhere north of Reno, Nevada. I don't remember exactly where it was or how to get there. You drove up a lonely 2 lane road then turned right into another 2 lane and finally got to an unmanned gated entrance. It appeared to be a renovated WWII army training camp.

We were not the only ones there, some other activity was happening beyond our area.

We spent 5 days in the classroom learning various aspects of winter survival. First lesson: Get as far away from the crash site as possible!

Many lessons including: How to use the various parts of your parachute for different purposes, how to live off the land. We spent 3 nights out in the forest doing night survival training, then 2 days in a simulated prisoner of war camp.

It was very cold in October, in the mountains north of Reno. We were the last group to go through the school in 1961 before winter set in. They stuck us into a long semi-circular hut, low to the ground about 5 feet high in the center. We had to bend over to find a spot on the gravel floor to sleep on. There were 2 pot- bellied heaters (wood fueled), one at each end. We wore thermal underwear under our flight suits and heavy parkas but boy was it still cold. I dozed for a while but they rousted us out of the hut in the middle of the night to do exercises. They also threatened us with another call out in a couple of hours to be hosed down with water. That never happened.

During the day, we were shown various forms of torture that the North Vietnamese used. The one that I considered worst was being stuffed into a rectangular box head first, closed up, total darkness. Your arms were pinned to your side, could not scratch your nose or anywhere else. No physical torture, just mental. I concentrated on counting forward to 100, then backward to 0. Tried counting up 500 and then back to 0 but it was hard to concentrate and say one hundred one, one hundred two…., up to four hundred ninety nine and five hundred, then four hundred ninety nine, four hundred ninety eight, etc. I tried sleeping while waiting for them to open the box. I am hoping that I never get shot down. Give the enemy just name, rank and serial number, easier said than done. It makes you wonder if you are strong enough mentally to withstand torture in a POW camp.

On the second night, we were taken to an obstacle course where we simulated escape from a POW camp. We crawled past a guard tower, crawled under barbed wire fencing with machine guns firing over our heads and finally escaped only to be caught and trucked back to camp.

In the morning, after lunch, we were briefed on the next phase of training, given maps of the terrain showing a marked location of a check-in point 10 miles away and the location of a safe camp 20 miles away. Paired in 2's, we had a 4 hour head start before being tracked by dogs and helicopters and told-----There's the mountains, run for it. You have 3 days to reach the safe camp.

The terrain was all hills, fairly steep. You climbed one hill only to find out that you had to go downhill to reach the next hill and climb it.

Darkness crept up on us, we stopped for the night. I gathered some fallen tree branches and brush, crawled under them to try to sleep. The next morning I had to crack the ice covering small streams to fill my canteen. We kept trucking. Up one hill, down to the next and up another. Around noon, we came to a small river of water, too deep to wade across. 8 others showed up, we debated whether to go upstream or downstream. 4 of us went upstream and the other 4 went downstream. After a short walk, we came to a wooden bridge across the stream and a parachute tent with a man sitting under it at a table. It was the check-in point, halfway to safety. We had covered 5 long miles with another 5 miles to go. He gave us each a beautiful, large orange. I've never eaten an orange that tasted so good, also directions to the safe pickup area on the other side of the bridge.

We stumbled along all afternoon and most of the night by moonlight, then decided to rest. I found a hollowed out log to crawl into and nap for several hours. We then continued on and finally came to a fence with an abandoned guard tower over it but, on the other side there was a huge bonfire, buses and crewmembers sitting around the fire. We crawled under the fence and arrived at safety. Welcome to freedom and food! Flight meals and drinks next to warmth around the fire, but best of all, buses to truck us back to the BOQ (Bachelor Officer Quarters).

After waiting for 3-4 hours, we loaded into the buses and headed back, leaving several buses to wait for the remaining tired, lost souls. After unloading, we got our personal gear from our rooms, loaded our separate cars and drove out. Finished! Back to Reno and civilization.

First of all, back to Sparks, Nevada to a Pancake House to load up on food. Lots of pancakes, bacon and coffee. It tasted really good! I had lost 20 pounds on the 20 mile adventure. Several years later, someone told me about the well- known, infamous Mustang Ranch outside of Sparks, where you could get rest and comforted by hostesses but I couldn't afford it nor did I have any energy left to enjoy it.

CHAPTER EIGHT

Fulfilling My Wish List

I drove to San Francisco to say goodbye to my Aunt Lily, Uncle James and family before driving across the entire country to my first assignment at Homestead AFB, Florida. I was assigned to flying in H model B-52 bombers as a navigator. Homestead AFB is just 20 miles south of Miami and close to the start of the Florida Keys. It is also close to the entrance of the Everglades National Park. What a wonderful start to my new life.

We waited 6 months for brand new airplanes to arrive from the Boeing Aircraft Company in Seattle, Washington. They were the last B-52's to be built. Crews arrived intact so I was a spare, just filling in and getting my flying time.

The Plans Section at the B-52 Wing in Westover AFB, Massachusetts asked for help. Being a spare, I was sent TDY (temporary duty) to them. With 5 days to get there, TDY pay plus travel allowance. Wow! A trip through so many places plus enough extra money to pay for expenses, I can't believe it. I loaded my car with food and clothing, checked out of the squadron, gassed up and headed north.

A. MIAMI TO SPRINGFIELD

I followed the coastline north through Jacksonville, Florida to Savannah, Georgia, then turned inland, still driving due north to Columbia, South Carolina. I decided to explore, see the Appalachian and Blue Ridge Mountains and the Shenandoah Valley. I will ultimately end up in Virginia not far from Arlington and the Tomb of the Unknown Soldier. I bypassed Kitty Hawk, where the Wright Brothers flew the first airplane but I'll drive down the coastline on my way home and stop there. 157 miles to Ashville, North Carolina to get on the Blue Ridge Parkway.

One of the folk songs that I really like is "Shenandoah". I have always thought that it was about a lover who had to leave his loved one to go across the Missouri River to work or settle. He really missed her for a long 7 years. It was romantic and sad. But in reality, the real origin of the song is different. Still romantic and sad, it was about a French fur trapper (voyageur) who came down the Missouri River from Canada, to trap beaver and collect their fur. He trapped on the western side of the Missouri River. He fell in love with the daughter of an Algonquin Indian Chief. He trapped beaver and didn't see her for 7 long years but he had to return home to Canada with the fur. It makes more sense that he paddled across the river to visit and spend some time in the tepee with her whenever he could. The long version of the song also mentions Sally.

I believe that he came down the river, trapped beaver on the western side for 7 years, got lonely and decided to take the fur that he had and go back to Canada. He was saying farewell to the Indian woman without seeing her and going back to Canada to hug and squeeze a woman named Sally. It is a sad and haunting melody that sticks in your memory.

Stopping at Ashville for the night to rest, I got on the Blue Ridge Parkway early the next morning. It was a spectacular drive along the crest of the mountains, more types of trees and bushes than I have ever seen and many lookouts to view valleys and mountains. I saw old log cabins that were built many years ago. The last 105 miles was driving on the Skyline Drive through Shenandoah National Park. If you appreciate scenic drives and beautiful views, this is a relatively little known treasure. It is totally different than driving up U.S. 1 along the coastline from Los Angeles to San Francisco, but just as memorable.

I came down off the mountains at Front Royal, Virginia and drove the 70 miles to Arlington, Virginia to spend the night. Nearing sunset, I drove over to the Tomb of the Unknown Soldier to pay my respects. I watched the tomb guard march 21 steps down a mat, turn toward the tomb, turn again and 21 steps back. The shouldered weapon is always placed on the shoulder away from the tomb to signify use against any threats. They are really sharp, specially picked and trained US soldiers. I said a prayer for all the fallen comrades of all the wars.

I drove the 10 miles into Washington D.C. early the next morning. It was Saturday and very little traffic on a cold and overcast morning. Stopped at the Lincoln Memorial, drove around the White House, looked across the water to the Washington Monument and stopped to look at the Jefferson Memorial. It is hard to believe that I am actually here, gazing at all these famous memorials and the White House. This is really an unplanned trip. I just happened to drive past Washington D.C. on my way north. What a great start to a great day.

Bypassing Dupont Circle, I drove northeast through Baltimore, Maryland to Philadelphia, Pennsylvania to find Independence Hall. I wanted to see the Liberty Bell housed there.

I followed the signs to Independence Hall and got to see the Liberty Bell. It was cracked, Oh Wow! I didn't know that. But also housed in the same room were several other surprises. On display under protective glass, on loan from the National Archives, were 3 other documents. This is my lucky day, I happen to be in the right place, at the right time. They were the original signed "Declaration of Independence, the Bill of Rights and Constitution of the United States". The afternoon went by so quickly. I wandered among the precious documents reading them. Maybe later in life, I will be able to bring my children to view these documents that started our country.

We read about and study these documents and the men who wrote them and signed them, but to actually see the original signatures of men like John Hancock, Thomas Jefferson, John Adams, Benjamin Franklin, etc. was humbling.

After spending the night in a local motel, I followed the words of Ben Franklin....... "Early to bed, early to rise, makes a man healthy, wealthy and wise", I got up early the next morning and headed out for New York City, 100 miles away. No coffee, just a full tank of gas and 5 hours of sleep.

I drove across the George Washington Bridge at 5am on a cold, overcast Sunday morning, drove down the west side of Manhattan following the Hudson River until I came to the ferry landing for the Statue of Liberty. I kept waiting for 2 hours for the first ferry of the day to the statue. It was cold. I ran the car engine for 10 minutes at a time to warm myself, got out and walked around did jumping jacks, everything to ward off the chill. I got back into the car to run the engine for another 10 minutes. Finally, there were people moving in the ferry.

Thank God, they sold hot coffee. I guess Ben never got on the road early in the morning or maybe he ate a later breakfast or had a wife who slaved all night to feed him so early. By the way, was he married? Were there little Franklins running around?

10 of us got off the ferry with great expectations of climbing up to the head and looking out, only to see scaffolding around the statue and a sign: "Closed for repairs, Scheduled opening next April". We tried to go back but the ferry had already left.

10 disgruntled people wandering around on an island with nothing to do but hope the ferry gets back soon. No palm trees, no coconuts, no native women au naturel to look at, only concrete and a gloomy cold day. Finally….the ferry.

I am still healthy, not wealthy or worldly, nor wiser. Maybe someday!

I retraced my route back past the George Washington Bridge and kept going, across the Bronx to the freeway heading northeast to Connecticut. I was so disappointed that I totally forgot about visiting one of the huge engineering accomplishments, the Empire State Building. All I had to do was make a right turn on West 34th Street and drive straight ahead for ½ mile to the tallest building in the world in 1962.

It was a perfect day for going up to the Observation Deck on the 102nd floor, be in bright sunlight then look down to see the street. But there was no street, just heavy, dark clouds dropping rain on everyone at street level. It is an unreal experience. Look up, bright blue sky. Look down, tops of gray clouds. It would be like flying in an airplane except you were standing in a building.

I drove through the city early on a Sunday morning. The streets were empty, no-one moving. I wanted to kick all the people responsible for my monumental screw-up but then I wouldn't be able to sit down for a month. Only 160 miles left to go, through New Haven and Hartford, Connecticut and into Westover AFB at Springfield, Massachusetts.

B.   NEW ENGLAND

Summer turned into early fall with the trees putting on a spectacular color show. I drove out to the Atlantic to see Plymouth Rock during the first free weekend that I had. They have crazy traffic circles in New England. I had to go around and around them 2-3 times before finally getting into the proper lane to get off. Just like Annette Benning in the movie, "The American President". She couldn't get off Dupont Traffic Circle in Washington D.C. on her way to the White House.

Plymouth Rock was a small rock, about 5-6 feet long by 2-3 feet wide. It is housed at sea level in a structure and protected by steel grating. Originally, it was about 15 feet long by 3 feet wide pointing due east. People chipped pieces of it to sell or keep as souvenirs, reducing it by 2/3 of its original size. It is the rock that the pilgrims stepped on when coming ashore from the Mayflower in 1620.

I drove back to Westover AFB in the afternoon, once again enjoying the beautiful multicolored trees.

Does the name "Springfield" sound familiar? It is the home of the Springfield Rifle Company and also the Smith and Wesson hand gun Company. The Merriam Webster Dictionary Company, Goodyear Tire Company and the Rolls-Royce companies are also located here. Plan to visit them next weekend. The game of basketball was invented here and also volleyball nearby.

C. RETURN TO CHAOS

The Cuban Crisis erupted during the last 2 weeks of October, 1962. I was recalled to Homestead AFB and didn't get to see the rest of New England. Per instructions, return immediately. I couldn't stop at Kitty Hawk on the way home or drink out of Ponce de Leon's "Fountain of Youth".

I returned to a strange scenario. No airplanes, no ground crews, empty as if abandoned. There were families and civilian workers but no hustle and bustle of a bomber air base. Our Alert Facility was occupied as a Command Post for a joint Army, Air Force and Navy strike on Cuba.

President Kennedy visited the Alert Facility and toured the air base in an open convertible. I stood with the housewives and children by the side of the street and waved as he slowly passed by, only 15 feet away from the President. Another unexpected item to add to and cross off my wish list. Seeing the President so close by, Wow! Unreal!

I lived just a short distance from the railroad track from New York to Key West and back. Normally, it transports fresh vegetables to the East Coast but now during this crisis, it ran continuously, day and night carrying Army equipment, troops, artillery guns, tanks, armored vehicles, etc. one way, to Key West.

We were amassing a huge invasion force to attack Cuba. Our nuclear attack force was put on alert to attack Russia, If they started any kind of conflict. 180 of the 1436 B-52's were on airborne alert with 23 orbiting within immediate strike range of Russia. 145 Intercontinental Ballistic Missiles with nuclear warheads were on ready alert and B-47's were put on ground alert.

Tactical Air Command deployed to the panhandle of Florida, 511 fighters with tanker and recce. aircraft support. Air Defense Command deployed 161 nuclear armed fighters to bases within 9 hours of Cuba to defend Florida. The Navy blockaded Cuba. It was decided that ground invasion of Cuba was overkill, we used intimidation as well as diplomacy to have Russia remove all weapons from Cuba. The Navy did not have enough landing craft to support a full sized invasion. Compared to Russia's limited amount of nuclear firepower, we had a massive amount of nuclear weapons ready to be launched at them. When they realized their folly, they shut down. We had 27,000 vs their 3600 nuclear warheads. Our very accurate delivery systems vs their very unreliable and inaccurate systems, Who's guns are bigger? Come on make my day!

They totally shut down and walked away.

CHAPTER NINE

Make Me Shiver

A. DELIGHT

All of our B-52's, aircrews, maintenance crews, support staff and equipment were moved to an air base in the Midwest, beyond the range of the middle range missiles being installed in Cuba. They sat on ground alert as well as their turn on airborne alert. Those of us left behind (flyers) were loaned to Ferry Command.

We were to ferry C-47's, (Gooney Birds) being given away to foreign countries. A huge gas tank was installed in the cargo section, it ran from the crew compartment to the tail. It also had a sextant port. I reported to the Ferry Command office and was instructed to check out a sextant and report in the morning to a small airfield outside of Miami. There I met the rest of the crew: pilot was a full Colonel from the Pentagon, co-pilot a Lt. Colonel from the pentagon and a sergeant to tend to the gas tank. We were briefed on our mission: Fly the Gooney Bird to Turkey with overnight stops in Bermuda, the Azores, to a small airfield in the south of France, Rome and finally Turkey. Leave the aircraft in Turkey, take a commercial flight to New York, transfer to another and home to Miami.

Wow! I'm absolutely delighted. I will get a chance to use a sextant and dead reckoning to get an aircraft across the Atlantic to Europe. The pilots had radio beacons to guide them but it was my job to get them within range of the beacons.

We stopped overnight at Bermuda and the Azores. Being a full Colonel, the pilot was able to persuade the reluctant motor pool into checking out a staff car with driver to drive us into town at each place to eat at a local restaurant. He then ordered the driver to drive around for a while before turning in for the night. No-one argues with a full Colonel.

On the next leg of the journey, from the Azores to France, we ran into heavy cloud cover and couldn't see a thing under us. No ocean, no land ahead, just the sun above us. I took sextant shots to determine our latitude and used dead reckoning to take into account the forecast wind direction. Off the coast of Spain, I determined that he had drifted north of course and instructed the pilot to turn 10 degrees right. He insisted that the radio beacon showed us right on- course. I didn't want to argue with a full Colonel but for safety sake, I had to. I brought my maps up to show him my position. We finally bet on who was right. If he won, I would buy him an expensive bottle of scotch when we returned to Miami and if I was right he would leave me in Paris. (He would teach this snot nosed young Lieutenant a lesson). The co-pilot reached up and turned the radio frequency of the radio beacon to another channel, it showed 10 degrees right. The pilot didn't say a word, turned 10 degrees right. Previously, when we landed in the Azores, the pilot and co-pilot had gotten into an argument. The co-pilot dropped his mechanical pencil on the floor and was looking for it. The colonel said forget it, let's go. After waiting 5 minutes for him in the staff car sent to pick us up, the Colonel instructed the driver to leave him. We went on in and the co-pilot had to hitch a ride in, on a maintenance van. He was pissed but couldn't say anything. The pilot was a Full Bird Colonel.

Well, the co-pilot got even by helping me. Rome would have been nice but Paris sounds great.

The major in charge of the small Air Force unit at the airfield told the Colonel that he had to use a navigator to help him cross Europe and showed him the regulations. The Colonel then pointed out the eagles on his shoulder board and said no, he was leaving me in France to see Paris. End of conversation.

The Major was a very kind person. He called for a staff car to take me to the railroad station, gave the driver some money to buy me a ticket to Paris, then reached into his pocket and also gave me around 20$ in Francs and told me exactly how to catch a cab from the train terminal to the military operated high rise hotel in downtown Paris. He also gave me the name of a Senior Master Sergeant at a desk in the hotel who would get me home to Miami. All of the money was from his own pocket.

Can you believe it? I am actually in France on a train heading for Paris. I boarded the train with just a sextant in a carry bag and a small Air Force issue duffel bag with some civilian clothing.

The train was a long, old, wooden type with many windows. It just had individual bench sets which became uncomfortable on the long trip to Paris. We start off in brilliant sunshine and rode through the countryside on a beautiful day. The train made many stops in smaller towns. As we approached Paris, the skies darkened and it began to rain. The fog moved in, making everything miserable. I followed the major's instructions and made it to the hotel and checked in. I then looked for and located the Senior Master Sergeant to arrange for my flight home.

He said: "Lieutenant, when your money runs out, I will put you on a commercial flight back to La Guardia Field in New York and on a connecting flight to Miami. When you're ready, just come and see me." What a great adventure, no hassle, no fuss.

My unexpected visit to Paris was a first in many ways. It was my first train ride, first time on an elevator, first time above the 2nd floor of any building (my room was on the 9th floor) and……..my first and only encounter with a bidet. The bathroom in my room contained 2 toilets, side by side. I used the one with a flush handle and then wondered why there were 2 toilets. This is France, the men and women must use the toilets together, side by side, holding hands. I sat on the other toilet and turned the knob full and got blasted with a stream of cold, cold water straight up my butt. Boy, did I stand up in a hurry, jump up and down, yelling and cussing.

That was cold and unexpected. You can't imagine what it feels like to have your bottom and vitals smacked with unexpected ice cold water. My twins, Hung and Low got a good washing.

Back into the bedroom to rest for a few minutes, in the middle of the bed was a small wedge shaped pillow in satin or silk covering. I leaned back on it, looking for a TV to watch, no TV in the room in 1962. The pillow was wedge shaped and too small and uncomfortable anyway. I finally decided that the maids had left her child's pillow behind by mistake.

I got on the elevator and went downstairs to look for something to eat. Stopped by the check in and told her about the maid's pillow. She laughed and laughed and finally said that it was used to raise a woman's bottom during oral encounters, and otherwise. There was one in every room. Oh, ok. As I walked away, I thought about it. You can kiss a woman standing up, sitting down and lying down. Why do you need a fancy wedge shaped pillow to raise her bottom? Maybe if you kissed a midget you would need it. Either France must have a large amount of midgets or there was a midget convention going on.

Looked at all the brochures and then wandered out the front entrance to see what I could see. Almost nothing, heavy fog had rolled in and you could only see 15 to 20 feet in front of you. Keeping the buildings to my left within sight I decided to walk around the block. I came upon a traffic light to my right with 3 beautiful women in fur coats standing there. They must live in the apartments to my left and are waiting for a cab. Continued walking around the block in the heavy fog trying not to get disorientated but I did. I regained my bearings when I passed behind the same 3 women still waiting for a cab. It must be a busy time for cabs or maybe they were waiting for a bus or late date. They waved and spoke to every car that stopped for the red light. They must have a lot of friends or business acquaintances. Learned later that they were paid professionals looking for business.

Second day in Paris. Still raining. A cold front had dropped in and became stationary. I had enough money left to buy a bus ticket on a tour bus leaving that evening. It was dark, gloomy, raining. Not Paris in the springtime, or gay Paree, or lover's paradise, just cold and depressing.

It was a short 3 hour evening tour of the West Bank. Starting at the Arc de Triumph, the bus drove down the Champs-Elysees, along the West Bank of the River Seine. Too dark and foggy to see and appreciate the tree-lined famous avenue, old buildings, palaces and gardens. We passed the Louvre Palace and Museum which houses the Mona Lisa painting and the Venus de Milo statue, Tuileries Gardens, Notre Dame Cathedral and also a shopping district containing the Chanel perfume outlet and factory. Saw a white church (**Basilique du Sacre-Coeur) off on a hill.**

We finally stopped for a drink at a smoke filled, dimly lit cabaret. We were seated at tables toward the back of the room, served small drinks while we waited for the 3 act stage show. There was no stage, just an area cleared for the performers at the front of the room. First a mime, then a male singer. Both received mild applause.. I couldn't

see them from my seat because the room was packed with a lot of men seated in front of us. The music started for the third act, a Can-Can dance performed on the floor by the 3 bar maids. All the men in front of us got up, whistled and cheered loudly and stomped their feet. I couldn't see anything through the men so I sat down. I was getting tired, a very depressing day.

The women seated across from me reached across the table and squeezed my arm saying, "Look! They're naked!" I stood up and tried to look between the men standing in front of me, saw a flash of legs and the music ended. I sat down, very disappointed. The woman reached over to console me and said: They weren't really naked, they just didn't have on any underwear". The bar maids were wearing very thin, white blouses and short red skirts. The Can-Can is a very revealing dance, raucous and seductive. Kick forward-legs high, bend over and shake your bosom, turn around and bend over, flip your skirt up. I missed all of it.

Back on the bus, the lady sat down next to me and we chatted for a while to pass the time since it was too foggy outside to sight-see. She was a divorced housewife from New Jersey on vacation. The bus went back up the West Bank to drop each of us at our different hotels. Mine came first very quickly. I got a glimpse of the Eiffel Tower across the river through the fog. Someday, I'll come back to Paris in the spring to see the Eiffel Tower up close, the flower gardens, the Louvre and more Can-Can dancing.

The next morning I went to see the Senior Master Sergeant about going home. He sent me out to Orly Field in a staff car with instructions to see another Senior Master Sergeant who booked me on a commercial flight back to Laguardia Field in New York. It was filled with military families returning to the US from Europe. My connecting flight to Miami was delayed until 4am. All the other flights departed leaving just us waiting for our flight. They moved us to another area with bleacher seats, dimmed the lights and closed the terminal. Everyone went home. We tried to sleep but the wooden seats were too uncomfortable. I was surrounded by a group of dentist returning to Columbia from a dental convention in New York City, around 1/3 of them were women. I didn't know that there were that many women dentist. We all tried to make small talk or read magazines but the light was too dim and we became very tired, tried to nap until 4am.

Finally our flight arrived, we boarded and got to Miami. Sunny and warm Miami! Said good-by to the Columbian passengers, they were only ½ way home and walked out into the bright sunshine. Wow! What an unexpected and fascinating adventure.

B.   WORRY

The Bermuda Triangle, is it fact or fiction? Is it a reality or a story made up by someone's fertile imagination? It is the area within a line drawn from Miami, Florida to Bermuda to San Juan, Puerto Rico and back to Miami, also referred to as the Devil's Triangle. Nassau and the Bahamas are entirely inside this area.

A writer, E.V.W. Jones, started the allegation of possible paranormal activity within the triangle in 1950 and others followed suit in 1952, 1962 and later. Many of the references were later researched and found to be either false or had happened elsewhere but the rumors of planes and ships disappearing in the Bermuda Triangle continue to this day.

I passed twice through the Bermuda Triangle on a training flight from Waco, Texas to Puerto Rico and back. On our "Gooney Bird" ferry to Turkey, we must have crossed into the triangle at least once as we flew right on the line between Miami and Bermuda. I didn't notice any strange happenings but knock on wood, we were lucky.

The Bermuda Triangle is a very fascinating subject. I have eliminated those air crashes and boats disappearing which happened elsewhere or did not happen at all and narrowed it down to some of the ones that actually did happen in the triangle.

December 5, 1945. At 2:10 in the afternoon, a flight of 5 Navy TBM Avenger Torpedo Bombers left Fort Lauderdale, Florida on a training mission under the leadership of Navy Lieutenant (captain) Charles Taylor heading due east into the Bermuda Triangle. They flew 64 miles to a bombing range halfway to Grand Bahama Island. The flight started their last bombing run at 3pm and then were to continue flying due east for 17 minutes, then turn NNW for 18 minutes, crossing directly over Grand

Bahama Island, then turn WSW for 31 minutes to arrive back over Florida around 4:06 to 4:10 pm, ready to land back at Fort Lauderdale.

The TBM Avenger has a range over of 1.000 miles, top speed of 275 mph, and can stay in the air for approximately 5 hours. This flight mission was scheduled to travel 365-400 miles for only 2 hours. Well within safe limits.

40 minutes after leaving the bombing range, Lt. Taylor radioed another Avenger flight coming into the bombing range stating that he had lost both his compasses and was flying over the Florida Keys. He was disoriented.

The leader of the other flight told him to fly NNE and he would reach Fort Lauderdale. A Navy investigating team determined that he had flown too far east and upon turning north, he passed Great Abaco Island and was looking at a series of small islands very similar to the Florida Keys. He was actually in the area where he should have been and should have turned into the setting sun for 31 minutes to arrive back over Florida. Instead, he assumed that the islands were actually the Florida Keys and if he flew NE, keeping the sun on his left wing, he would reach Fort Lauderdale. This sent him out to sea. He wandered back and forth in the Bermuda Triangle NE of Grand Bahama Island until his last transmission at 7:05 pm and then ran out of fuel and ditched. The wreckage was never found.

The strangest part of all of this is what possessed the Lieutenant, being disoriented with both compasses out, not to abort the mission and fly into the setting sun for home? It would have brought him out of the Bermuda Triangle and over Florida where the airfield towers would have guided him home. Was he possessed by aliens?

He was an experienced pilot with 2500 flying hours in Avenger and similar aircraft. The standing rule was "If in doubt, turn 270 degrees into the setting sun and fly back to land". The sun was setting due west, no compass needed. To further complicate matters, why did the other 4 Avengers flown by students with at least 300 flying hours follow him all the way to the sad end? At least one of them was overheard advising him by radio to turn left into the setting sun.

To add to all this confusion, one of the 2 PBM Mariner Seaplanes sent to rescue them exploded in mid-air. It took off at 7:27pm, radioed in at 7:30 pm that all was fine, and was never heard from again. The Navy investigators concluded that it had exploded, cause unknown.

<u>December 28, 1948.</u> A DC 3 carrying 29 passengers flying from San Juan, Puerto Rico to Miami, radioed that it was 50 miles South of Miami, 20 minutes from landing. It was never heard from again. The plane was never found.

<u>March, 1918.</u> During WWI, the USS Cyclops, a massive carrier ship, left Brazil in February with a load of coal and 10,000 tons of manganese ore. It also carried 309 passengers. The ship made a stop at Barbados for additional coal and supplies, leaving there on March 4 heading for Baltimore, Maryland. It was scheduled to pass through the **Bermuda Triangle (entering it 600 miles North of Barbados) and arriving in Baltimore on March13. It was never heard from again, no wreckage found along its entire route.**

<u>**January 30, 1948.**</u> **The first of 2 disappearances that bankrupted a new airline company in England. Star Tiger was a 4 engine propeller driven passenger aircraft, Tudor IV. It was flying from England to the Azores. At 3:15 am the aircraft called and received a radio bearing from Bermuda, the captain gave their ETA as 5am. They were never heard from again. A search could not find a trace of the airplane. No aircraft, 31 souls lost.**

<u>**January 17, 1949.**</u> **Another Tudor IV named Star Ariel took off from Bermuda headed for Jamaica at 8:41 am, estimated ETA Kingston 2:10 pm, ETA to 30N checkpoint, 9:37 am. At 9:37 am, the captain radioed that he had arrived at 30N and was switching frequencies to MRX, Kingston. Kingston never received his transmission. No-one heard from the aircraft again, the Star Ariel did not reach Jamaica. Visibility was excellent that morning, radios were fine. 20 souls disappeared with the aircraft.**

Two Tudor aircraft searched for Star Ariel. One flew along her route from Kingston to Bermuda and the other flew from Bermuda along her route to Jamaica doing a lattice search pattern. Dozens of ships and aircraft searched for days, nothing found.

Because of the two mysterious disappearances, future passengers cancelled, causing the company to go bankrupt. The Civil Air Ministry of England suspended use of the Tudor aircraft. It was a

nice 4 engine prop., passenger aircraft with no problems other than in the Bermuda Triangle.

<u>February, 1963.</u> A tanker, the SS Marine Sulfur Queen, carrying a load of molten sulfur, left Beaumont, Texas with 39 crew members aboard heading for Norfolk, Virginia disappeared off the southern coast of Florida. Some debris was found off Key West but no trace of the ship or its crew.

I've picked 2 very prominent theories to write about. <u>They make the hair on my neck rise!</u>

<u>Time portals</u>
I am not a sci-fi fan, nor a Star Trek "Trekkie".

My knowledge of time portals is very limited. Apparently, within the Bermuda Triangle, there is a mile and a half wide corridor which compresses and expands like an accordion, 25 times per year for 28 minutes. If you happen to wander into this corridor during this period, you will be trapped. When the portal expands, you are ejected into another time portal somewhere in space. This time portal is linked to many others throughout the universe. Aliens use these portals to transport themselves to other planets, including ours. They use time compression, solar power and friction reduction to travel throughout the universe. They may or may not look humanlike, like the green human creatures in the Mel Gibson movie "Signs". They may look like you and me.

<u>Underwater Pyramids.</u>

In 1970, Dr. Ray Brown, a naturopathic practitioner was scuba diving in the Bahamas when he got separated from his friends. While searching for them, he came upon a strange pyramid shaped underground structure. Its surface was mirror smooth but he found an entrance with a narrow hallway leading to the center of the structure. There he found a small rectangular room with a pyramid shaped ceiling. The room was well lit and hanging down from the top (apex) was a metallic rod with a faceted red gemstone attached to it. The bottom of the gemstone was pointed with the point facing directly down to a crystal sphere nestled in a pair of cupped, bronze colored, burnt hands sitting on a stand. Nothing was removable except for the 4 inch diameter crystal sphere. He took the sphere and got out of the pyramid. As he exited, he heard a voice telling him never to return. Underground pyramids are associated with time portals. Their locations are close to the time portals.

Looking down into the sphere, you will see 3 pyramids in decreasing sizes. Looking at the sphere from the side, you will see thousands of tiny fracture lines, no images. From another angle, some people have seen a human eye staring serenely at them. Metals become magnetized when placed next to it, compasses spin wildly. Some people have felt strange tingling when standing next to it and other a wind blowing.

Dr. Brown first exhibited the crystal at a psychic seminar in Arizona and only a few times after that. Unfortunately, it is not available for public viewing.

Brain- Washing.
There is possibly a third theory which fascinates me. It is scary.

The aliens really don't need to leave the Bermuda Triangle to take over this country. Cruise ships go back and forth between Florida ports and Nassau and the Bahamas. The largest cruise ship carries 3,600 passengers. Over 10 million cruise passengers pass through Florida ports every year aboard one of the cruise ships headed for Nassau and the Bahamas, right in the Bermuda Triangle.

If the aliens boarded each ship and brainwashed everyone on board, in 20 years they would have brainwashed over 200 million people without even leaving the Bermuda Triangle. The population of the U.S. in 2013 was 315 million people. They would look and act normally except when they hear the code word: "Calabash Cousin" (an example of a code word) they will then automatically go to their assigned waiting areas and receive advanced alien weapons and sent to destroy their assigned targets.

Think about it! 200 million people attacking us from within with alien weapons. That would be the ultimate surprise! Do you know anyone who went on a Caribbean Cruise? You might want to keep an eye on them. At least find a place where you can hide from them if necessary.

Forget that I told you about flying on a training mission from Waco, Texas to Puerto Rico and back. Also, that we flew from Miami to Bermuda on our way to Europe, straddling the edge of the Bermuda Triangle. Nothing happened to us that I could tell, really. We are perfectly normal. Knock on wood!

C.   WHEN SPARKS FLY

The time went by so very quickly at Homestead AFB. I made trips to the Northeast and Paris, The Cuban Crisis happening 90 miles away, a cross country road trip to San Francisco at Christmas with stops at Carlsbad Caverns, Nogales, Mexico to watch the bullfights, A military hop to post-war Tachikawa AFB, Japan, 3months TDY to Maxwell AFB, Montgomery, Alabama to attend Squadron Officers School, there were also many attractions around Miami to see. I visited both world class horse race tracks (Hialeah and Gulfstream) greyhound dog racing, Jai Alai, a Miami Dolphins pro football game, and watched Chubby Checker do the twist at a new Peppermint Lounge that opened in Miami.

The Everglades National Park was close by, watched alligators sleeping in the shallow water. Their eyes followed you. And, many different types of birds. I bought a rod and reel and tried to fish off the bridges along the road leading to Key West, no luck but it passed the time. Last but not least, Miami Beach. Its white sand beaches were only 18 miles away.

The dog races were very weird. Sometimes the dog that you bet $2 on just stopped and wandered off the track to pee or investigate something that caught his eye or just got tired of chasing a fake rabbit.

I also tried to attend a Russian Language Class at the University of Miami. The instructor was a 30 year old Russian woman with nice legs. She sat facing us in the front of the room with her legs crossed.

It was hard to concentrate but If I got shot down over Russia, it would help to know some of their language. Could not finish the class, it got too hard to learn the words. Besides, she might have been a spy sent to watch us.

After a short 19 months, 15 B-52H model flights, I was reassigned to Dyess AFB, Abilene, Texas. Strategic Air Command (SAC) decided to form a brand new B-52E model Wing there and drew air crew members from its other bases. Unlike Homestead AFB where all the crews came in intact, only some of the crews were already formed. We had to wait for our airplanes to arrive.

From July to December, 1963, I had to drive back and forth to Roswell, New Mexico to practice flying in their B-52E model bombers. Driving back from Roswell on November 22, 1963, we heard a shocking announcement over the radio. President Kennedy was shot while riding in a motorcade through downtown Dallas, Texas. Of all places, Dallas, only 180 miles East of Abilene. Really sad news, he was a good president.

San Angelo, Texas.

On one of my off weekends, I happened to drive down to the nearest large town, San Angelo. There I met a young couple from Goodfellow AFB who were being reassigned overseas. They were having their car repaired and needed a ride so I helped them. In return, I was invited to a going away party being held for them that night. The wife conveniently positioned me at a table next to a single, almost divorced woman. Someone to talk to, I never intended to form a personal relationship but things happen and I dated her for 5 to 6 months. She had 4 children, Pamela, William, Ronald and Teresa. The eldest was a beautiful, intelligent 16 year old daughter, next, a 13 year old mischievous son who loved to tinker with anything that he could get his hands on, and then a 12 year old son, quiet and determined to stay out of trouble and sight but made a major mistake, he followed his brother around and was punished for the same trouble that older brother often got into. The fourth child was a pretty 2 year old girl with very fair skin. She was not quite what you would call mulish, only very obstinate. I left all discipline and training to Dorothy, my future wife. We got married on September 19, 1964.

After a beautiful honeymoon trip to San Francisco, we bought a house in Abilene and settled in for a long stay. But, SAC calls again with the first of many changes.

D. THE SAC SHUFFLE

I was the first navigator to sign into the bomber wing at Homestead AFB and the first to leave. History repeats itself, I was the first to sign into Dyess AFB and the first to be reassigned.

We were sent to Caribou, Maine, to Loring AFB located in the far northeastern corner of the US, 10 miles from New Brunswick, Canada.

Wow, cold country. Get the car ready for heavy winters, buy warm clothing and shoes. Being stationed so far north gets to be very expensive. We also bought a pop-up pull along sleeper to help with the travel expenses. We only spent 6 months in our new house in Abilene before we had to sell it.

On the road again, this time with a family to look after. First stop, Castle AFB, Merced, California for several weeks of ground training in B-52G model aircraft operations and then, weapons school.

Then, a long 3500 mile, 7 day road trip from the Pacific to the Atlantic and then, up to the northeastern tip of the U.S. We didn't know what to expect, but we were young and capable of facing anything.

We spent hours poring over a road atlas, marking the spots we could see on this long journey.

First, the Grand Canyon. What a wonderful way to start. Leaving Merced early in the morning, we reached the campground in the Grand Canyon National Park around 5 in the evening. We set up the camper, ate a bite then drove over to see the beautiful natural wonder close to sunset. It was beautiful, in all its colors and glory. Hoped to see it again the next morning but the fog rolled in and we only got glimpses of it before we left.

Next stop, Meteor Crater. 40 miles east of Flagstaff, Arizona. Meteor Crater is a very large hole in the ground, 3900 feet in diameter and 570 feet deep, created by a meteorite strike around

50,000 years ago. The meteor is estimated to be 160 feet wide traveling at a speed of 28,000 to 45,000 mph.

Most of the meteor vaporized upon impact but on display at the Visitors Center is a 1400 lb. meteorite fragment plus other specimens. Meteor Crater is privately owned.

Next, moving along eastward, 70 miles to Petrified Forest National Park. This was really a surprising stop. We expected to see logs turned to gray colored rocks lying around. We saw logs lying around that were brownish colored on the outside and cut by a high powered chain saw into equal segments. The logs had turned into solid quartz on the inside, colored all colors of the rainbow by impurities in it. They were not actually cut apart but broken into equal segments by an uplifting of the earth in this area, amazing. They sparkled in the sunlight. Wow! The area became a national park in 1962, just 3 years before we saw it. It also includes a part of the Painted Desert.

It was time to continue moving eastward, times a wasting, daylights burning. We found a campground between Gallup and Albuquerque, New Mexico and set up for the night.

Long days and short nights, we have some large cities to drive through, Albuquerque, Amarillo, Oklahoma City, Tulsa, St. Louis and Indianapolis in the next 2 days. We spent our 3rd night on the road at a campground between Oklahoma City and Tulsa, 4th at a nice, shady campground besides a small river, approximately 2 miles past St. Louis.

The St. Louis Arch was 3/4th completed with 2 high arches facing each other high in the air, programmed to meet each other within inches. In my opinion, it is one of the truly amazing engineering feats. It will be 630 feet high with an observation section at the very top. You ride up a closed in tram swinging to stay level, like a ferris wheel seat or a gondola. Bring your lunch with you, If the tram should stall it may take hours for help to arrive. Like the Eiffel Tower in Paris, it will be a beautiful sight. It will be an American landmark that people will always remember.

Rolling on the 5th day through some large cities. Indianapolis, Indiana, Columbus, Ohio, Pittsburgh, Pennsylvania and Buffalo, New York. Familiar names, they all have NFL football teams except for Columbus.

Finally, only another 21 miles to Niagara Falls, honeymooner's destination. We spent the night there, our 2nd honeymoon but this time with 3 children along.

It was a cold night. The oil heated furnace in our room was not working properly. We did lots of snuggling to stay warm but definitely not a honeymooner's night.

Niagara Falls was beautiful. We stood in the mist from it and watched the water cascade down and disappear below us. You can actually feel the power of all that water flowing over and down. Our jackets were too light, our skins too thin to be standing around for very long. Maybe we can come another time without the children, find a better motel to stay in and totally relax, let our hair down. Just like our first honeymoon.

Half frozen and tired, we continued across the top portion of New York. So far, we've driven from California to New York, across 11 states with only 3 left to go Massachusetts, Rhode Island and Maine, 14 in all. Reached Albany, New York in 6 hours, another 3 hours to Boston, around Boston and finally on to Portland, Maine. We arrived there in the evening at suppertime.

At a roadside restaurant, we ordered 2 lobsters and watched them boil them for us. Maine is famous for its lobsters and potatoes. Before French fries became very popular, Maine led the nation in potato production. We took the take-out meal of 2 boiled red lobsters, potato salad and corn on the cob out to a picnic table overlooking the Atlantic Ocean. Now, what in hell do we do with the lobsters? Got out a hammer and 2 pliers from the car, Bill and I proceeded to attack the hard lobster shells. We finally got the meat out and ate it. Not a very satisfying meal but a unique one.

On the 7th day of the road trip, we drove the remaining 5 hours to Limestone, Maine and into Loring AFB in the far northeastern tip of the US. We were 5 miles from the Canadian border. Loring is the largest SAC base and also the nearest SAC bomber base to Russia.

Our stay at Loring AFB lasted one full year before Sac decided to move our entire squadron to Plattsburgh AFB in upstate New York. Aircrews, B-52 bombers, maintenance personnel, equipment all made the move.

While at Loring, Bill and Ron managed to spend a week gathering potatoes for pocket money. They also skated on a homemade ice rink created by the other families in the buildings in our large square of buildings. They flooded the area in the space between us. The base also had a ski slope but we never got a chance to see it before moving to Plattsburgh.

In June of 1966, we made the move to Plattsburgh. Each family had pre-assigned base housing. We drove down to Bangor, Maine, then headed west on US highway 2 through New Hampshire and Vermont to a car ferry at Burlington, Vermont. We crossed over Lake Champlain on the ferry to a landing just 10 miles south of Plattsburgh, New York.

Plattsburgh AFB was a wonderful assignment. Sheltered by the Adirondack Mountains, the winters were moderate and summers cooler. I was on a crew selected to compete as one of 2 crews in the competition for the SAC Bombing Competition. We did very well. My navigation was very accurate, our bombing excellent but the other crew had a slight edge and was selected to go to the competition.

As a consolation, we were sent to Beale, AFB in California. Waiting for our transportation from the parking area into de-briefing, we watched 2 U-2 aircraft take off, circle the airfield, then head almost straight up and disappear. Awesome! Our high flying spy planes.

We arrived at Beale AFB around 4pm on a Friday and weren't scheduled to leave until Sunday at 5pm. The co-pilot had a friend stationed at Beale, who loaned a Volkswagon Beetle to him on Saturday. I don't see how it was possible for 5 of us to fit into the little car but we did and off we went to Sacramento, 40 miles to the south.

We stopped at a winery to taste their samples and buy some wine. Next stop, South Lake Tahoe, 100 miles away. In 1966, it was a quiet, small resort area. Our lodging was a 2 story wooden building with a small casino on the first floor including a restaurant and stairs to rooms on the second floor. It was a pleasant stay, everyone treated us like family. I remember crossing the quiet street, walking through pine trees and suddenly seeing a beautiful blue, blue lake. The smell of the pine trees, crisp, cool morning, fresh air and the blue lake sticks in my memory as one of the most beautiful scenes that I have ever encountered. We left after breakfast, headed back to Beale AFB and flew a training mission back to Plattsburgh.

While at Plattsburgh, we went to visit the World Fair in Montreal, Canada. There were large displays in individual pavilions by many nations. It took us 2 days to go through almost all of them but little Teresa got tired of walking so we stopped. I can't remember what we saw in each display but they were so huge, it took us at least an hour or two to try to see what they had in each display.

We also visited Lake Placid, home of the US Winter Olympic training facility and Winter Games. It was spring, not much happening there on a non-Olympic year. We walked partway down the Olympic Toboggan Run. Without snow and ice, it looked very bare and not very impressive.

Once again, the dreaded SAC shuffle happened. I would have loved to stay there for 4 to 5 years, but we were only there for less than a year. This time, the 6 newest navigators to sign into the squadron were selected to be loaned to Tactical Air Command for training in RF-4C fighter reconnaissance aircraft. We were to become navigator/camera operators in the back seat of the fighter. We were headed for the war in Viet Nam.

On the road again, back across the country to Mather AFB in Sacramento, California to attend 2 months of RF-4C ground school. It was mainly about equipment and how to operate them. The instructor was a friend and roommate at Bombardier School. We had classes all week with weekends off.

The transition from flying in bombers to flying in a fighter was both exciting and fearful. Every flyer wants to fly in a fighter but going to Viet Nam and getting shot down was always in the back of our minds.

On the weekends, we explored the surrounding countryside. We drove out to Placerville and Coloma, camped at roadside parks along streams of water and panned for gold in the streams. The water was very shallow and went around boulders of rocks. Panned upstream, behind the rocks to see if there were any nuggets of gold trapped there. Between us, we found 8-10 small pieces of gold but don't know if it was real or fool's gold. It was fun, an escape from the military life.

Next, back to Texas for RF-4C flying training at Bergstrom AFB in Austin, Texas. I flew 38 training missions at Bergstrom AFB from

August, 1967 to November, 1967. 14 were night training flights and 24 day training.

The RF-4C is a very stable aircraft. Unlike other aircraft, you don't land it by slowly floating down to a gentle landing. Instead, you point it down in a designated glide slope and speed and drive it into the ground. It was designed to land in a very small space on an aircraft carrier. You drop a tail hook which engages a barrier bringing you to a screeching halt. Early in my training, the instructor pilot flying the airplane demonstrated the stability and sturdiness of the RF-4C by flying down the base leg, putting the aircraft into the proper glide slope and speed. Turning into the final approach, he put his hands above him onto the canopy. The plane landed itself.

There was also an instance of an F-4C aircraft flaming out (losing both engines) with the pilot ejecting safely, and the plane then landed intact in a pasture.

In the 3 months of flight training, we practiced many things. Among them: Low Level Flying, both day and night, popping cartridges at night to illuminate the target to be photographed, aerial refueling with KC-135 tankers, both singularly and in pairs, taking the barrier with our tail hook down, etc.

One of the memorable flights was a high speed run with an instructor pilot. We took off with no external fuel tanks and headed straight out to the Gulf of Mexico, made a 180 degree turn and accelerated on a run straight back to Bergstrom. When we passed Mach 1, the airplane vibrated a little, we watched the Mach meter pass Mach 2 then backed off and did a straight-in landing with minimum fuel. Wow! Earned my Mach 2 club pin, I actually flew at Mach 2.

I finished the intensive training in early November, 1967 and prepared to leave my family and go to war. They settled for a year in San Angelo. I then caught a hop on a military aircraft from Abilene to report in to Travis AFB, Fairfield, California (approximately halfway between San Francisco and Sacramento). We were then bussed out to Hamilton AFB (30miles north of San Francisco) to Weapons School for 2 days of training.

We practiced firing the M-16 rifle in single shot, semi-auto and burst modes, then went indoors to take it apart. They darkened the room to total darkness and we had to put it back together. It wasn't easy. Watched a demonstration of bazooka firing and got to lob live grenades over our heads. It was an informative and enjoyable few days. We then bussed back to Travis AFB where we awaited transport to Clark AFB in the Philippine Islands.

I met 2 navy lieutenants at Travis and we hung together while waiting. We were headed for Jungle Survival School in the Philippines.

Arriving at Clark AFB, there was a 5 day delay before the next class started so we moved out to a hotel outside the base. The hotel was owned and operated by a retired Filipino Colonel who fought in WWII against the Japanese and remembered General MacArthur. Whenever we left the hotel, he sent an escort with us to interpret and protect us. We had to check into the base every day. At night, we were invited to visit with him for a drink. He told us about his experiences during the war. The hotel was protected by a 10 foot high wall with a gate kept locked at night. Security guards were on duty 24 hours. It was a protected compound.

Jungle Survival School was easier for me than for others. The Philippines has the same climate and foliage as Hawaii, I felt right at home.

The best and certainly most needed experience was practicing a live helicopter pickup. Each of us took turns directing a rescue helicopter into a pickup area, as close as possible to a position directly over us. We also practiced getting into a rescue harness.

The school ended with escaping into the jungle and hiding from patrols. Everything felt subdued because the next stop was going to the bases we were assigned to for flying into combat.

Said goodbye to my 2 navy Lieutenant friends and boarded a flight to Bangkok, Thailand. I reached there the last of week of December and got on a bus to an orientation area where we received lectures on the dangers of venereal diseases, what to encounter in the jungle as well as towns. Learned of a little green snake which hung from branches in the jungle, its bite was lethal. Death occurred inside of a few minutes. No King Cobras or pythons in this area, thank God!

Spent the night at a military run hotel for Officers downtown and then caught a flight to Udorn, Thailand the next day. Udorn is located 300 miles north northeast of Bangkok and 40 miles south of the western extension of Laos.

At Udorn AFB, a sponsor from our squadron was assigned to take me around the base. He took me down to the Recce squadron to meet the Squadron Commander, assigned a locker, over to supply to get issued a vest and flying helmet and to room assignment. The next day, I had to get a complete physical. I also had to carry a giant vial of hepatitis serum while walking around from building to building, filling out paperwork, etc. I must have walked a mile from building to building. The serum had to be defrosted to room temperature, it was frozen. Hurry up, stick it in my butt and be done with it. Tired of hearing all the jokes about how much it hurt, how it was a pain in the ass.

I was assigned to stay in a group of small rooms, 4 men to a room with only space for 2 double bunks and 4lockers. There was one group bathroom in the middle of the building to shower, shave, etc. Of the 28 men in this building, 16 were shot down. It was not very good odds of staying alive.

The sponsor took me downtown to visit all the shops. You had to sharpen your bartering skills and not take the first price. They then gave you a glass of Thai beer to soften you up as you brought them down to half price. Some people could get lower but I could only afford to buy one or two items so I settled for half price. I bought a decent Seiko watch for myself. I am now sorry that I had not bought a 35mm camera. Memories captured on slides are priceless.

On the third day upon arrival, I flew my first combat mission with an instructor pilot. It was a weather reconnaissance out to the ocean over route pack 1, up the coastline to route pack 3 and back down the water to route pack 1 and South Vietnam and home. We encountered heavy clouds throughout the entire mission, couldn't see the water at all. We broke out into the open for a few minutes over the water and saw an Aircraft Carrier. we were headed right for it. It looked dime sized, how can anyone land on it? Unable to contact them to say we were friendly, we banked off toward land and barely missed the barrage of gunfire from their escort destroyer. Wow! What an exciting first mission. Our second mission was a simple mission over some of the roads in Laos, flying at tree top level to check for enemy movement of trucks and supplies during daylight hours. Then, on our third mission, we were sent out of the frying pan and into the fire. We were sent to route pack 5, to Dien Bien Phu.

CHAPTER TEN

Combat Flying

A. RF-4C

After Dien Bien Phu, I flew the next 20 combat missions in January and February, 1968, into route packs 1, 2 and 3. On one mission, we flew up the coastline taking side looking radar photos of the road along the coastline. On my 24th mission we flew into route pack 6 (the most dangerous route pack) to take photos of the Nguyen Steel Mills located approximately 35 miles north of Hanoi. The pictures showed that the steel mills were completely destroyed, only rubble remained in the huge area that it occupied.

The next day, the squadron had a meeting of all available flyers. Tactical Air Command had asked for 3 volunteers (navigators from fighter aircraft, specifically from our squadron) to move to the Forward Air Controller Wing for a test program using the starlight scope at night to see trucks moving down the Ho Chi Minh Trail. Flying in an unarmed, slow moving Cessna spotter aircraft was extremely hazardous duty. They were among the most respected flyers. The Squadron Commander asked for volunteers and I volunteered to be one of the three navigators. Why not? Flying in an unarmed RF-4C was also hazardous duy.

B.   CESSNA O2A

We caught a ride on an empty helicopter returning to NKP (Nakhon Phenom) air field, 150 miles east of Udorn on the Mekong River.

At NKP we entered into a whole new life, a different way of Air Force living and flying. The Forward Air Controllers and the Air Rescue flyers were the most respected of all the combat flyers. We flew in small, unarmed Cessna aircraft directing strikes into ground targets and Air Rescue picked you up if you got shot down. We both had to have a fearless attitude, just do our jobs, ignore the ground fire. Avoid the fire but above all, locate their positions and bring in all available, heavy, fire power to destroy them.

Normally, the enemy on the ground realized that we could do that and did not show their positions by firing on us.

We were assigned single rooms in new buildings made of teak wood, with window air conditioners. A total contrast from what we had at Udorn. We walked everywhere.

There were no pre-flight briefings or planning. The squadron published a weekly flying schedule, areas to be covered, what time for each FAC. The parking and taxi area was made of steel ramps laid down on the ground and the runway, a packed dirt take-off strip. Nothing paved, just simple and efficient. Each FAC was assigned to his own aircraft.

I flew mainly at night but during the day, I was invited to fly with the day Forward Air Controllers. They showed me what they checked and looked for during the day. It was dangerous during the day, you were a visible slow moving target and you couldn't see the ground fire coming. At night, the enemy used tracer bullets in their 37mm guns and you could see a volley of bright tracers seconds before they reached you. Duck!

The FAC pilots did their best to make us feel at home. They were not proud or vain, just guys doing their jobs. We complemented them at night using the starlight scope. It is a giant telescope with light gathering capability. If there is a little light available at night, perhaps some moonlight or bright starlight, you were able to see shapes and figures. It cost $6,000 and was approximately 2 foot long and 5 to 6 inches in diameter. The army uses them on perimeter patrol.

Our night flying Cessna O2-A aircraft were painted black with the door removed on the passenger side. You buckled into the seat and made sure it held. In the air, the pilot banked the airplane so you could lean out and look under the aircraft using the scope to survey the road. We carried and dropped burning marker logs that burned brightly for around 3 hours. They were used to guide the fighters into where we wanted them to drop their bombs. We also carried flares and smoke rockets. "Rocky Two, Two, you hit one kilometer south of the marker, the trucks are now passing the marker. Cleared to come on in, drop just a tad south of the marker, Rocky Two, Two". And so it goes. We chased trucks up and down the Ho Chi Minh Trail for 4 hours each shift, every night.

The trucks normally pulled off the road into a designated shelter during the day. Captured truck drivers when interrogated said that the shelters had food and telephone service. They were handcuffed to their trucks, no escaping.

Later in the war, listening devices were dropped to spy on enemy movement but the nerds that devised this plan didn't realize that the enemy wasn't stupid. They just picked up the devices and moved them elsewhere to transmit erroneous information. We were sent on many goose chases only to find nothing. They built an empire out of this with much publicity about how good and important they were. Electronic surveillance cannot replace someone personally looking at the targets. It's like buying anything on the internet. The picture and descriptions look wonderful, it will certainly improve your life. Reading user comments may change your mind about it.

Estimates reported in the Stars and Stripes weekly say that the Viet Cong moved 500 to 1,000 trucks down the Ho Chi Minh trail on a busy night. We destroyed only 5 to 10 percent of them. The only way that you can prevent this is to stop them at their source. Take a rolling invasion force with air support and roll north, kick their butts.

One moonlit night, the enemy pulled a surprise on us, something that none of the night FACs had ever seen. The Viet Cong set up a trap for us. They located 37mm guns in a rectangular pattern with 4 guns on each side of the road and 2 guns on one end of the box. When we passed the full moon they all fired. 10guns with volleys of 7 tracer bullets each. Man! Surprise, surprise, they are serious about trying to kill us! 70 bullets, headed right for us. We were just coming down the road slowly looking for trucks, one last time before our shift ended. All of a sudden, the sky exploded with bright orange and red tracers. If the series of 70 tracers had almost no brightness or if you saw only 1 tracer with no tail, look out. Duck! The shot was coming right at you. If you just saw the tracers, don't fly into them. All of the pilots that I flew with had instinctive reflexes, they ducked instantly, almost before I knew what was happening. It was crazy. Thank God for good pilots. We just happened to be the first aircraft that they unloaded on.

We had 20 minutes left of our shift, it was prudent to wisely pull off to the side, have a cup of coffee while we collected our senses. We then briefed our incoming replacement on what happened. Heading for home, lived another day. Everyone was put on instant alert. Fighters, navy A-6 bombers from the aircraft carrier, all ready to get some action supporting the next FAC. The guns didn't fire again that night.

We encountered the same trap once again on another night. The FAC that we were replacing had just finished bringing in air strikes to destroy a convoy of trucks coming down the road at sunset. He estimated around 18 trucks were in flames on the road. An RF-4C in the area requested permission to come on in and photograph the damage. He was given directions on the location of the trucks and cleared to come on in. We flew parallel to the activity waiting to relieve the FAC.

The RF-4C proceeded down the road and started popping cartridges that lit up the ground and himself. The standard procedure was to pop only 3 carts maximum and no more. He continued to pop 9 total cartridges, allowing the Viet Cong to fire, reload and fire again. It was a miracle that he was not hit. The enemy is there, no time to be careless.

It was a spectacular display of fireworks, no-one told him what danger he had escaped from. We were all too stunned by what we had witnessed. Needless to say, we avoided that part of the road during our 4 hour shift. We warned the incoming FAC of the trap but they did not fire again that night. The 37mm guns are portable. We were normally only fired upon by 2 or 3 guns but not by 10 all at once.

Flying with the day FACs was hot and a lot of times boring. Using stabilized binoculars, we looked at everything that might hide equipment, troops, trucks hiding under trees, etc. But, sometimes it was very exciting.

On one day flight, we noticed large bulky piles covered by tarps placed under trees a short distance from the road. Barely visible tire tracks led to them. We flew down to tree top level to see what it was. It was a huge stockpile of petroleum barrels. We called for all available firepower to hit it, every fighter on call launched to help us. The fighters normally made 2 passes dropping the bombs that they carried and headed for home. Sorry guys, I'm at Bingo Fuel (fuel necessary to get home plus an emergency supply). See you next time FAC. Navy A-6s were the most accurate and stayed with us longer than the others. As strike after strike came in, 37mm guns on a hill behind the stockpile started to fire at us. Also, the enemy brought in anti-aircraft guns to add to their defense.

We were beyond our minimum fuel and it was getting dark so we had to leave. Heavy smoke and flash fires filled the area as well as explosions as the barrels lit up. I believe we destroyed most of the stockpile. We both were awarded the Distinguished Flying Cross for **staying with the attack under heavy fire. Fighter came and dropped their bombs and left. We stayed for 4 ½ hours flying around and around the** target assessing damages, location of the enemy guns and directing strikes back in. The night FAC that replaced us called in strikes against the guns and destroyed them.

On an early morning day flight, I flew with another pilot to check on an army team that was dropped off on top of a steep sided hill with a flat top. It was similar to a mesa in the southwest US. One of our FACs led a chopper in to drop the team off at sunset the night before. Unknown to everyone, the Viet Cong had moved in a division of troops at the bottom of the hill at the same time. At sunrise, they began to climb the hill.

The army team consisted of an army captain leading 20 Laotian soldiers. Their job was to cut the enemy phone lines and harass the enemy wherever they could. This time, they were trapped before even getting started with their work.

We arrived on top of the hill and made contact with the Captain. His voice was high pitched as he screamed for help. The Viet Cong soldiers had almost reached them. We called for any slow movers in the area and anyone with napalm bombs. 2prop fighters came right away and strafed the area to delay the soldiers climbing the hill and then the fast movers came in with the napalm bombs. They destroyed the entire side of the mesa. You could hear the enemy screaming in the background when we talked to the Captain, everything was burning. He had calmed down and said that they were ok, thanked all of us for our help. The team went down the far side of the mesa and went to an alternate location to be picked up. They lived to see another day.

We met many officers from many groups at the Officers Club. Some of our pilots talked to the Special Forces Team stationed in a compound a short distance from us. Their job was to train the Laotian teams before sending them back into Laos. The Captain we had saved invited our entire squadron to a BBQ in their compound. They flew in 75 T-bone steaks, 40 cases of beer, 40 cases of soft drinks, chips, etc. They got anything that they asked for. They were Army Special Forces, supported by some high ranking generals.

We learned that each Laotian team was led by an army captain with 20 Laotian soldiers under him. When they were picked up around 10 days later, the captain normally returns with only 5 or 6 survivors. The rest of the Laotian soldiers were killed.

After flying 16 missions at NKP in March, 1968, I was sent to Pleiku, South Vietnam to fly with the FAC squadron there, over southern Laos. They picked up coverage where we ended flying from NKP and continued south to the Cambodian border.

Pleiku sits on a high plateau in the central area of South Vietnam. We lived in empty army barracks with bare concrete floors, no air conditioning, an army cot for a bed, a locker and a wooden crate for a nightstand. I had to walk to a central building for a shower and to use the bathroom. We were a lot better off than the Army Big Red Division who lived not too far from us in large tents. Walked up the hill many times to the Officers Club only to find that they were closed, not even coffee available.

There wasn't much activity in southern Laos. We checked an intersection of the road heading due south into Cambodia and a road leading east from it into South Vietnam. There were abandoned gun bunkers on both sides of the road at the intersection. They were always empty. Following the road east to South Vietnam we were fired upon by 55mm guns. We flew at 6,000 feet, the maximum range of the 55mm guns is 5,500 feet. The shells exploded just below us, They looked like popcorn, popping puffs of smoke.

At the end of my 6 week stay at Pleiku, during which I flew 31 missions in March and April, 1968, I was flown to Bangkok for 3 days of rest. Glad to get away from the raw conditions at Pleiku. That was rough living.

In Bangkok, I ran across a fellow trainee at **Bergstrom AFB, Texas. His plane was shot down in southern Laos at the same intersection that we had checked several days ago. The bunkers were empty. The Viet Cong had moved portable 37mm guns into the bunkers and shot down an unsuspecting RF-4C coming leisurely down the road and** banking left to follow the road into South Vietnam. Both he and his pilot successfully bailed out but he saw his pilot get killed by ground fire while floating down. He bailed out first, landed some distance away and was picked up by a rescue chopper before the Viet Cong reached him. His tour was over, he was being sent home.

Back to NKP, May thru July. For 6 weeks in August and early September, 1968, I was sent to Phan Rang, South Vietnam to establish a Navigator Forward Air Controller program at the Forward Air Controller School. We did well as night observers so Tactical Air Command decided to send us more navigators to work into the program. It was more of an attitude adjustment for most students. They had to learn to be fearless and follow what the pilots were trying to do. To say: "Hell with everything. Let's destroy these supplies moving into Viet Nam to be used against our soldiers!" I didn't tell them that the pilots did things on the spur of the moment. They would notice something moving under a group of trees along a small stream. "Let's go down and check it out". "Roger, pilot, do it!" Move away to hide our intentions and then come back flying up the stream of water at almost eye level with a group of trucks stopping to take a break. Everything went so fast, it seemed blurry to me but we saw their astonished, surprised looks as they reached for their guns but we were already gone.

I was awarded the Bronze Star for establishing a successful program.

The FAC instructors were a loose bunch of guys. We drank a lot of beer and cokes, enjoyed sitting around and talking. Everyone helped each other. A total contrast from the RF4-C flyers at Udorn.

One day, the commissary had no beer or soft drinks. The Squadron Commander sent a pilot and myself in a spare 02 airplane down to Tan San Nhut AFB to get some. We followed the railroad tracks most of the way there, through some very large rubber tree plantations. We passed some large plantation houses, just like those in the south in pictures I've seen. Also passed an orchard of papaya trees. At Tan San Nhut, we taxied right up to the commissary, loaded cases of beer and cokes, then taxied over to say hello to a FAC unit there.

It never dawned on me that there were large rubber tree plantations in Viet Nam formerly owned and run be the French during their occupation of the country.

I flew 15 missions with the instructor pilots at Phan Rang before returning to NKP in the middle of September, then flew 5 missions at NKP before returning to Udorn to finish my year tour of duty with the RF-4C fast movers.

At Udorn, I flew 15 missions in October and November in the RF-4C finishing with 120 combat missions in the RF-4C and Cessna 02A. Enough combat missions to last a life time. Your life expectancy dropped drastically as you flew more missions beyond 100, few survived 200 and almost none 300.

CHAPTER ELEVEN

Chief of Intelligence

I asked to be assigned to Hawaii or Japan as my next assignment. I received an assignment to Yokota AFB, Japan to work on the staff of a large triple F-4 Fighter Wing.

A. YOKOTA AFB

I received a 5 year tour of duty, leaving in December, 1968 after attending Sea Survival School at Homestead AFB, Florida. This was the last of 3 Survival Schools offered by the Air Force. I previously had gone to Winter and Jungle Survival Schools.

We drove out to Travis AFB, California, dropped off our car at a facility outside of the air base. We were allowed to ship a car for our use in Japan and they took care of shipping it for us. I was able to bring my family to Yokota AFB. We got there on Christmas Eve.

We lived off-base while waiting for base housing. I rented a wooden, small, 3 bedroom house from the Japanese. There was no insulation in the walls, it was cold, drafty. The bathroom had a Japanese furo (wooden, water filled tub) which you used for bathing. You soaked and washed in hot water which was heated by an oil furnace. You had to fill the tub with water and light the oil heater prior to use. The normal procedure is to wash before getting in to soak, keeping the water clean for the next person. There was no space to do that in the small room, besides the house was cold. If the tub was larger, you could take a bath as a family and all get clean at the same time. Wash each other with soap and get into the tub but it was only large enough for one person to sit in it.

We finally got base housing at Tachikawa AFB, 20 miles from Yokota in military housing. I commuted to work at Yokota where I eventually became Chief of Intelligence for the fighter wing. We basically built and controlled Top Secret target folders for the fighters who rotated into Osan, AFB, South Korea to sit on nuclear alert. Yes, fighters also carry nuclear bombs.

With Mt. Fuji in the background, we loved it there. We made several long trips to see the countryside on our leave days. On the weekends, we packed a picnic lunch and drove to see the local sights. Cherry blossom trees in bloom, Up to the base of Mt. Fuji, etc. We sometimes shopped in the large concession store on the base for local items.

On a week- long vacation, we drove down the coastline to Nara. We stopped to watch nude women diving for pearls, I tried to appear not too interested, can't say the same for Ron. He wandered off to look for sea shells. We visited an old castle, watched a sumo wrestling tournament, stayed at a local inn with tatami mats on the floor and futons for cover. I don't remember all the details of this trip but it was fun. It was very relaxing. In Nara, we stayed at a hotel in a park like area, mowed lawns under a lot of trees. There were small deer wandering around, they allowed you to pet them. The people at the hotel gave us food to feed them. We loved it there.

One of my memorable experiences was going to pick up our car at a storage facility outside of Tokyo. It took several months for the car to be shipped by boat to Japan and stored in a large warehouse complex. I was given specific directions on how to get there, what to do and how to drive back. Early in the morning, I boarded a slow moving, old country train which stopped at every small town along the way.

After a long ride on wooden seats, I took a cab to the storage area. Riding with the wild and crazy Tokyo cab drivers is an insane experience that you never forget. They go everywhere that there is an open lane. In an empty lane of cars coming at you in the opposite direction, across 3 lanes of oncoming cars and up on the sidewalk behind people waiting at the curb for buses, etc. And he wasn't driving very slow either. I flinched a lot, even had to look away a few times.

Much earlier in life, as a bachelor in 1963, I caught a hop from Abilene to Travis AFB, California and then another to Tachikawa AB,

Japan for a week during the Christmas break. I walked out the gate into town to see post war Japan. Had a few beers but forgot about the 6pm curfew at the air base. They closed the gates until 6am in the morning. The bartender saw my predicament and made a phone call. A young local maiden came to take me home to stay the night with her family. It was very cold and we cuddled under a heavy futon together, trying to get warm. Her parents had a separate area behind some rice paper screens but her sister joined us under the futon clinging to each other for warmth. We slept on the floor on a hard tatami mat. The next morning, I woke up stiff and sore from the hard floor. The weight of 2 other people lying on top of me pressed me into the mat. Her parents brought us something to eat and some hot green tea. It was then time to walk back to the air base. A new experience for me but so cold in December, I couldn't enjoy it. Just grateful that I didn't have to spend the night in the bar.

Since I'm here, why not see the big city of Tokyo? Caught a cab to downtown, walked around for a while and tried to find a place to eat lunch. I could not read the signs, didn't understand what each shop was selling, didn't see food anywhere. Walking in a huge crowd of people, not understanding what they were saying, it was total confusion. Just noise. Enough, already. I'm lost, confused, hungry and tired.

Finally saw a cab and drove back to Tachikawa Air Base in it. I almost got a heart attack riding with that crazy cab driver but we made it back safely only to find the air base closed again.

I walked back to the same bar and told the bartender what had happened. He brought me a beer and something to eat. He made another phone call and another maiden, older but fuller built than the first woman came to get me. She generated more heat. I finally got warm. Still got a sore butt from laying under a heavy futon on a hard tatami mat.

What a wild and exciting experience for a young bachelor on vacation.

We brought a Buick Riviera to Japan. On our trip to Nara, the waiter who served us in the hotel dining room was fascinated with the car. I showed him all the features of the car. Several months later, I received a phone call from a mysterious Japanese stranger. He wanted to buy the car and asked what price I wanted to sell it for. I quoted the price I had paid for it and added $500. We agreed to meet outside the gates to the air base on Sunday. He looked at the car, handed me a sack full of yen, waited for me to count it. I gave him the keys and we both walked away. I think he must belong to the Japanese Mafia. Anyone willing to hand you $5,500 in yen, no paperwork, no questions asked must belong to the underworld. Or maybe he was a counterfeiter.

In the middle of our tour at Yokota AFB, Tactical Air Command decided to disband the fighter wing. Airplanes, aircrews, staff members and maintenance personnel were all transferred out to other bases. I was assigned back to flying on B-52s at Barksdale AFB, Shreveport, Louisiana. Back to the SAC shuffle. From being Chief of Intelligence of a large fighter wing to flying as a navigator again was a hard pill to swallow.

The movers came to pack all of our belongings in a large walk-in crate, inspected and sealed by a friend who worked at wing personnel, and flew back to Travis AFB, California.

As a favor to an old friend from navigator school, I brought back 2 sets of matched pearl necklaces for a dentist's wife. In return, she rented a room at a nice motel outside of the air base and met us at the terminal to drive us there. The next morning, we caught a cab to San Francisco International Airport. We then flew to Oklahoma City where a representative from an auto dealership in Weatherford, Oklahoma met us. With the money that we received by selling our car, we were able to order a new Buick Riviera at a huge discount. It had all the accessories that we wanted. The car was there, ready to be picked up.

After several weeks of visiting relatives and a trip out west to enjoy driving the new car, we drove out to Shreveport, Louisiana.

Shreveport is a commercial city in the northwestern corner of Louisiana, far away from Cajun country and New Orleans. In 1971, not a whole lot of excitement happening, just normal living. We had a house built for us in a subdivision among the tall pine trees, 5 miles from the air base. They filled our yard with rich soil, perfect for growing roses. We planted 56 tea and floribunda rose bushes and Saint Augustine grass plugs which filled in to create a beautiful lawn.

Barksdale AFB is a rather large air base. There were oil wells on the property beyond the landing strip and a wooded area. I was assigned to flying B-52, G models.

CHAPTER TWELVE

Rolling Thunder

A. ROLLING THUNDER

My enjoyment of living in a newly built house among tall pine trees lasted 5 months until April, 1972. SAC deployed our entire squadron to Guam to join the Viet Nam war by flying combat missions known as Rolling Thunder from Guam. Our wing had 3 squadrons. One squadron rotated into Guam, one flew airborne alert and the other flew training missions. Only G models B-52s flew from Guam. Modified D model B-52s also flew from U Tapao, Thailand.

Our bombing missions lasted 12 hours in flights of 3 airplanes. Each bomber dropped 84-500lb. bombs or 56-750lb. bombs or a combination of both. We dropped them into designated rectangular boxes in North Viet Nam or in support of our troops in South Vietnam. Approximately 200 bombs dropping on one target from just one flight, a lot of fire power. Observers on the ground say that it was very scary but a welcome sight.

We flew for 3 months and rotated back for 1 month of rest. We returned to Guam in the middle of August, 1972 for approximately 2 more tours of 3 month combat flying.

B. LINEBACKER – II

After peace negotiations with the North Vietnamese stalemated in early December, 1972, President Nixon and the Joint Chiefs of Staff gave SAC permission to launch the largest air attack since WWII. A massive launch using 207 B-52 D and G model bombers dropped payloads of 500, 750, and 1,000 pound bombs on targets in and around Hanoi and Haiphong in route pack 6 for 3 days with bombers taking off every 10 minutes in cells of 3 airplanes each from Guam and U Tapao, Thailand. It was an impressive sight to watch as we waited for our turn to launch 3 days later.

I flew on the third night. Target—the same Nguyen Power Plant that we photographed flying in RF-4Cs. It was completely flattened in January, 1968. In 5 years, the North Vietnamese had completely rebuilt the power plant. It was time to flatten it again. Our cell dropped 250 bombs on the power plant and immediate area and I imagine subsequent flights did the same.

The SAC planners at SAC headquarters, far, far away from the bombing in Omaha, Nebraska assumed that we could not handle flying into a heavily defended area so they used WWII tactics, the same way every night. We used the same altitudes, airspeed and time of night for 3 straight nights with an immediate turn to the west after bomb release into a 100 knot headwind. It left the electronic countermeasure equipment facing away from the ground radar. Flying 100 knots slower at the same heading, same time every night, with no electronic countermeasures put us extremely vulnerable, sitting ducks. What 5 year old child planned this attack? By the third night, the enemy knew exactly where we were coming from, exactly what time and what altitude. They just pointed their SAM missiles and guns in that direction and elevation and waited for us. We lost 8 B-52s these first 3 nights of the attack and 15 total bombers in the 11 day attack. Other aircraft which supported us were also lost.

President Nixon extended the 3 day bombing campaign until we accomplished complete control of the air space and destroyed all our targets. I flew 5 missions during the 11 day attack.

We shut down for a 36 hour Christmas break during which the piss poor planning by the SAC headquarter planners was reluctantly turned over to 8th Air Force planners on Guam who took the advice of very vocal crew members.

On December 26, 120 bombers were sent in on a one-shot mission. Approaching targets from different direction than before, at different altitudes, at different times and exiting out to sea. We were supported by 113 tactical aircraft which provided escort fighters, chaff dropping, Wild Weasel SAM hunters and added electronic countermeasures jamming the enemy radars.

The North Vietnamese air defense was overwhelmed and confused by the massive amount of aircraft flying in from all over the place, by the huge amount of chaff laid down by the tactical aircraft to hide the bombers on their radar screens. Only 68 SAMs were fired, hitting 2 B-52 bombers.

Due to the change in tactics by the 8th Air Force planners on Guam we were able to take control and put the enemy on the run. We continued bombing for 11 days until President Nixon ordered a halt to the bombings above the 20th parallel, Hanoi and Haiphong.

The war ended on January 27, 1973. We continued to bomb Cambodia, Laos and South Viet in support of ground troops until the end of April. I flew 82 combat missions in the B-52G for a total of 202 combat missions in 3 different types of aircraft. A total of 1200 combat flying hours.

I was sent to Loring AFB, Maine in April to upgrade to bombardier. Flew 10 training missions then returned to Guam as a bombardier. We flew training missions around Guam until the end of October when our entire squadron deployed back to Shreveport, home.

The war left a bitter taste in our mouths. We flew combat for around 9 months, dropped a lot of bombs, proved we gained "Peace with Honor", brought our POWs home and yet in the end, we lost South Vietnam.

The politicians are always hell-bent to prove that we are not a land grabbing, tyrannical power. When we have the enemy on the run, we ease up, not finish it. We let them back in to sway everyone with their smooth talking ways.

Instead of winning wars, we stalemate. We could have occupied all of Germany in WWII and told Russia to stick it and not even held a secret meeting, agreeing to split Germany. We could have overrun North Korea, taken Baghdad in Desert Storm, rolled north to the Chinese border in Viet Nam. We always have to pretend to act humanitarianly when finishing the job is in the best interests of everyone.

We give in to the smooth talkers, political analysts and lobbyist and newspaper hounds to back off so we look good as a humanitarian power. As a super power, by far the strongest in the world, we should take control and not give in. We make the rules and not some pencil pushing, ass licking politician or office worker. So much for my views on how to handle fighting wars. I say really beat them so they will not come back on us later. The war will end in weeks or months with less casualties on our side. Jump on them, pin them down until they say "Uncle! You win, I'll follow your rules". Not back off and say "Ok. Let's talk about it".

It is easy for people sitting around at home to voice loud protests and criticisms but put them in jeopardy of losing their lives, let them get shot at and they will sing a different tune. We protect their way of living.

CHAPTER THIRTEEN

K.I. Sawyer AFB

After 7 months of flying as a bombardier, I was promoted to Lieutenant Colonel and put in charge of the Target Folder Section of Wing Intelligence. I was back on the staff again.

We lived for another 2 years in Shreveport before the SAC shuffle caught up with us again. We were assigned to K.I. Sawyer AFB, Michigan. It is located on the far top of Michigan, not far from Canada. K.I. Sawyer AFB is around 15 miles south of Marquette and Lake Superior. Actually there were huge lakes all around us. Lake Superior 15 miles north, Lake Michigan 45 miles due south and Lake Huron about 120 miles east south east. Names you read about in Geography class.

It was beautiful country, far away from crowded cities below us, but…..very cold! Temperatures dropped to -40 degrees with the wind chill much worse. Everyone had a closed circuit television which broadcast every morning messages on whether it was too cold to go in to work or get out of the house. A snow vehicle with tank like treads carried hospital emergency personnel to the hospital. We used snow blowers to clear our driveways, our cars plugged into electric block heaters in the garage.

Long icicles hung down from everything, you were tempted to stick out your tongue and lick them. You would be there for a long time trying to scream for help. Your tongue or bare anything, stuck to the ice like glue. If you are male and tried to pee outdoors, be very careful.

We lived in a duplex house on the dead end of a street. The snow plows pushed the snow from the street to the end of the street, just passed us, 15 feet high or more. Our 2nd car, a little TR-7 parked on the side of our garage was buried in the snow all winter. It actually snowed there in July.

Coming from the South, we were not used to having a basement. Our washer and dryer plus a lot of storage boxes with our belongings were down there and a small workshop for me to develop my film from dot's Kodak camera. Some of the other families used their basement as another bedroom and I suppose others used it as a man cave.

I volunteered to run a Christian youth group for grades 6 through 8. We started with 8 youngsters, increased to 16 the following year and when I left 3 years later, there were 56 signed up for our group. The youngsters were a joy to work with, really hated to leave them but I had to get out of the cold country and make a new life for us in a warmer climate away from SAC.

We finished by taking the youngsters to a day of games and a picnic at a secluded lake with no-one around. Finished the day by sitting under the tall trees at sunset and singing "Kumbaya, My Lord". It still brings tears to my eyes to think about that moment. We never heard from the children again, I hope we made a difference in their lives.

In October, 1979, we left K.I. Sawyer bound for warmer Texas. We left 20 years of military service behind us—retirement. No more uniforms, short haircuts, involuntary moving. Freedom!

CHAPTER FOURTEEN

Retirement

A.   PECAN ORCHARD

A Year before retiring, we visited San Angelo, Texas to look for a property on a river where I could build a house and eventually build and establish a Christian Youth Camp for all denominations. We searched for over 2 weeks before finally buying a18 ½ acre property on the San Saba River with 1600 pecan trees growing on it. 20 of the trees were fully grown and producing nuts, the remaining trees were about 8 to 15 feet high and growing. Depending on their variety, the trees were spread 24-35 feet apart in horizontal and vertical rows. There were 16 varieties of pecan trees planted.

We hoped that eventually the pecan crop would support the youth camp.

It will be hard work, but we were young and eager to get started. Retiring from the military at age 42 had its benefits. I spent the long winter checking out books at the base library at Sawyer. Read and studied all that I could on how to wire a house (electric), plumbing, siding, sheetrock, how to roof a house, how to lay tile, etc. On Guam during Rolling Thunder, I passed a correspondence course on Interior Decorating. Some of the basic lessons helped in building and designing the house, drawing a blueprint of the interior for the lumber company to rough frame the interior.

In October, 1979, we finally did it. We said goodbye to upstate Michigan, said goodbye to the cold north and hoped that we would never have to go north again.

We headed south to Texas and warm temperatures. My toes curled up and everything perks up at the thought of basking in the warm sun again.

We bought a used mobile home to live in temporarily while I built a house. Moved it onto the highest part of the orchard, next to a bank, 20 feet above the river. Installed a septic system, electricity and ran a pipeline into the river to pump water for our needs. We lived there for a year.

I hired a local lumberyard to lay the concrete slab, rough frame the house and deck the roof. They ran the plumbing in the concrete slab. I then tiled the roof to have a water proof area to store all the supplies.

Installing the outer walls came next, then the doors and windows. Toilet, basin, sink, bathtub, sheetrock, etc. were all hauled in from San Angelo before closing the walls. Just bringing in all the supplies was a major job and took many trips with my pickup truck. We somehow accomplished it without out any outside help. Installing the outer walls came next, then the doors and windows, plumbing, electrical wiring of the entire house, sheet rocking inner walls and the ceiling, installing the house water cooler and heater ducting and insulating the attic. I finally got to tiling the floors, hauling in kitchen cabinets, building countertops and shelving and installing the heater, water heater and other appliances. Painting the inner walls was probably our last large project.

It was a lot of unfamiliar work but very rewarding to know that we could accomplish it. It was fun to watch the house come to life.

We moved all of our furniture and belongings into the new house in September, 1980.

Tending to the orchard needs was more than a full time job. Starting in February, I trucked in bags and bags of fertilizer from San Saba, 40 miles away. The area pecan buyer made a phone call and got it for me at a large discount, I bought around 3,000 bags.

It was exhausting work, they loaded the fertilizer for me, I then drove back and unloaded the bags. Don't remember how many trips it took but no rest for the weary. This was February, time to spray 1600 trees for bark problems. Moving quickly into March, it was time to spread the bags of fertilizer, 2 bags to a tree around the drip line.

Starting in April, I went into a 2 week work cycle. Mowed 18 ½ acres for 3 straight days, watered all 1600 pecan trees for 4 straight days, sprayed all the trees for three straight days, went to the commissary at Goodfellow, AFB, San Angelo for one long day of shopping for groceries, supplies and visiting relatives. I fixed pipes for 2 days and worked on the house for the remaining day of the 2 week cycle. The next day, it started all over again. I worked on the house during the watering days in between the morning and evening watering circuit of the orchard, turning rows of individual faucets on and others off using a small 3 wheeler.

Watering the pecan trees was accomplished by running a large pump down rails to a platform next to the river and pumping water to the orchard through a large 10 inch PVC pipe which ran down through the center of the orchard. Smaller feeder lines ran sideways from it to each water faucet at each tree. It all added up to 4 miles of underground water pipes, both PVC and black roll piping.

It was endless hours in the 100 degree Texas sun, digging up pipes which were leaking and repairing them. I turned very brown, like I was a sun tan machine fanatic or accidently fell asleep under the sun tan lamps.

Thank God the water faucets were 1 ½ to 2 feet off the ground. Sometimes rattlesnakes coiled around the base of the tree or even around the pipe to get cool. I had to come back with a hoe and chop them to pieces. I hate snakes and got carried away, uttered a few choice words or phrases to help with the task.

Starting in the middle of September, harvesting the pecan nuts started until just before Thanksgiving Day. The older pecan orchards waited until the hulls of the nuts dried out and it was easy to shake the nuts out. They used large tree shakers to shake the trees with the nuts flying down all over. Some of the larger orchards used special machines to pick up, sort out the hulls and leaves and bag the nuts. All of these machines cost a lot to buy or rent. A lot of orchards hired a company to do it for a percentage of the crop.

We had no money to buy or rent the machines and couldn't afford to just take a percentage of the crop. Instead, I hand -picked the nuts in opening hulls, standing on an 8 foot ladder in the back of my pickup truck and throwing the hulls with the nut in it into the back of the pickup. I averaged picking 400 pounds of nuts every day from sunup to 6pm. We then had to spend 2 hours extracting the nuts from the hulls and dry them on a concrete floor. I took a shower, ate a bite and went to bed.

I got up at 4am to rake the drying nuts around, had several cups of coffee and the harvesting started all over again.

One great advantage of doing this was that we could get the dried nuts to the buyer earlier than the other orchards and get top dollar for them. In the middle of November, the price dropped from $1.00 per pound to $0.35 cents per pound. We were able to get our full crop in to the buyer before the price dropped out.

As the trees grew large, the crop got larger. We started with 300 pounds the first year and reached 20,000 pounds 4 years later with the estimated crop to be 100,000 pounds in another 2 to 3 years.

The previous owner (a retired high school agricultural teacher who started the orchard) showed me how to select and prepare the best nuts of each variety for entry in the County Pecan growing Show. In 4 years, we won 82 ribbons (32 1st places, 30 2nd places and 20 3rd places). All the winners (1st places) were automatically entered in the Regional Pecan Show and all the 1st places there were entered in the State Championship Show. We won 9 championships (6county, 2 regional and finally, a coveted State Championship in 1982). We sold the orchard prior to harvest in 1983 and were not able to compete that year.

Winning 5 out of the 6 county championships in 1982 did not sit well with the local people. Only a few came up to congratulate us or shook our hand. I didn't see any of them out in the 100 degree heat working day after day to be successful. They weren't out in the freezing cold harvesting pecans either. I did, I earned every award the hard way.

Dorothy's dad became ill and she and Teresa (youngest daughter) moved to San Angelo to help her mom care for him. Teresa got married and went her way but Dot worked during the day and helped her mom at night. Pamela (oldest daughter) helped relieve her when she could. I was left to tend to the orchard. I harvested the entire 20,000 pound crop by myself.

Since we had no funding for equipment to harvest large crops, we decided to sell the orchard and give up our dream of building a youth camp. It became very lonely just living by myself and working so hard every day, I was glad to sell it.

I moved to San Angelo on Halloween Day, 1983 and rented a house close to her parents in a housing area north of San Angelo. In July, 1984, I ran across a house large enough for us on almost an acre of land. I bought it and we settled in.

B.   GEM CUTTING

Stepson Bill, got into the lucrative emerald buying and selling business. He flew down to Colombia, bought faceted emeralds from the locals and sold them in Los Angeles for a large profit. He gave me an old Facetron, Faceting Machine, some books on faceting, faceting laps and some small roughs to practice on. I started from scratch learning how to facet gemstone in the winter of 1988. I practiced 6 hours per day in a small, very cramped 5X8 room. Used a small electric heater for heat in the winter and sweated up a storm in the summer. When polishing a stone, the humidity had to be below 22%. I had to run a de-humidifier to drop the humidity from 33% to below 22%. It made the room very hot. No-one tells you how to bring the facets in just exactly right so that they meet properly. It takes hours and many days to learn the hard way how to do it. You must also use a very bright light illuminating the gem stone and a headset with various magnifying lenses to see the facets up close. I slowly began to learn and perfect my techniques. I wondered if I would ever be any good at this hobby.

I joined the 4,000 member American Society of Gemcutters in 1989. Took and passed a 200 question exam in 1990 and scored 98 on their gem cutting test, enough to be certified as a Master Gemcutter. The test was cutting a given design published in their monthly newsletter, to their specifications. You needed 97 to be given this award. In 1991 I received a score of 99.9 in my cutting and was certified as a Supreme Master Gemcutter. You needed a score of above 99.7. There are only 54 out of 4,000 members who have achieved this rating. Your cut facets were measured by a laser beam down to .01 mm. You needed a steady hand, perfect conditions and luck to cut all of the facets to this exacting standard.

As I cut the many different patterns and designs, I made mistakes. The mistakes showed anomalies that could possibly create a new pattern of reflections. I started to create new designs based on what I had accidentally run across. Won my first major Pinnacle Award in 1992 for a design I called "Wildflower". Won again in 1993 for "Blossom", In 1994, received an Honorable Mention for "Octandria", 2nd place in 1995 for "Indian Attack" and finally a 1st again in 1996 for "Falling Star". The competition was stopped in 1997. The Executive Director and founder of the society, Jerry Wykoff, had a massive heart attack. He organized all of the Societies work as well as wrote and published our monthly magazine. Everything stopped, we all truly miss him. I designed another pattern and called it "5 Star General". It was featured in a monthly magazine and used as the design for a gem cutting contest.

I was forced to stop cutting gemstones in 1998 due to rheumatoid arthritis in my fingers and joints. I could no longer bend hunched over the faceting machine for very long or hold the roughs steady on the laps. As a Supreme Master, it became my life. It was not easy to walk away.

C. RETROSPECT

All of my energy had gone into gem cutting. I was left with only mundane day to day work. We went to Las Vegas once a year for a change of atmosphere, play a little roulette, get up late with no chores, no worries, ate at their large buffets until they became very expensive.

The years went by so quickly with no major accomplishments except for 3 memorable experiences.

We went to Las Vegas and joined sister Elaine and her husband George on a bus trip to the Indian Glass Walkway extending over the Grand Canyon. I reserved it on the wrong day of the week. It was the day that the tourists from China visited Las Vegas, hundreds of Chinese tourists who paid a lot of money to come all the way to Las Vegas. There were at least 50 to100 on this particular day. They were all around you. You could look down through your feet and see the canyon far down below but that was about it. I wanted to lay face down on the glass floor, spread my arms out and say "Look ma, I'm flying". But, not today, it was too crowded. It was a one of a kind experience, walking on glass out into space. Before we rode the bus back to Las Vegas, the Indian hosts served us with a nice picnic lunch.

Elaine, George, niece Andrea and her husband Phil, came to visit us in April, 2005. We took them on a trip down to Brady, Texas to see the bluebonnets in full bloom and Texas long horn deer. I was 2 months away from having prostrate surgery and didn't feel very joyful but Pam and Teresa helped us with everything. We planned another visit but had to cancel because of sickness.

In 2007, accompanied by daughter Pam and her husband Donald, Dot and I fulfilled a dream of mine, seeing Lake Tahoe again. It was at the top of my list (visiting places that I enjoyed seeing before or want to see or missed).Now referred to as a "bucket list".

I will always remember walking through the pine trees and suddenly seeing a beautiful blue lake in 1966. The crisp early morning air, the smell of the pine trees, the chirping of birds in the still of the early morning was awesome. It was quiet, beautiful, enchanting. 41 years later, civilization had encroached on Lake Tahoe. Large casinos, winter ski runs, summer boating, parasailing, biking, hiking trails, golf courses, camping, ice skating, etc. Any form of recreation is here or will be here.

We rode around the lake on a large paddle wheeler. It was fun, a nice way to see the lake. Being the end of summer, it was windy and chilly on the lake. Changing memory cards on her camera, Pam accidently dropped it. 400 pictures gone forever, no-one volunteered to retrieve it in the clear blue water, 400 feet deep.

2 ½ days is not enough time to see very much. We drove around the lake with Pam navigating the 180 degree turns and the rest of us sight-seeing. She looked strained and exhausted from the effort when we got back to the hotel. I'm glad she did, better than I could have. One week in the late summer will be more appropriate. It was a unique, fun trip.

CHAPTER FIFTEEN

Windows of Opportunity

After returning from Lake Tahoe in 2007, I decided that at age70 my life is far from over. It was time to remove all encumbrances. Speaking figuratively, hike up your skirts, roll up your pant legs and go for it. There are very interesting areas to be explored, things that I've always wanted to learn about, but didn't get a chance to. 3 areas come to mind: Human Anatomy, Computers and Massage Therapy.

A. HUMAN ANATOMY

I've never learned about the human body. Being a man, having looked at my body for over 70 years, it is quite familiar to me. On the other hand, it would be very enlightening to learn about the female body, how it looks without any clothes on and how the different parts work. I've never looked closely at the intimate parts.

Having married a divorced woman with 4 children, I've never been close to a pregnant woman, seen a baby being born or even looked through a glass window at all the newborn babies being attended to by nurses.

Today, we have the internet with all the knowledge you wanted to learn. Web sites to order instructional DVDs, web sites to read about it or watch videos explaining the text or read opinions of others.

No need to get dressed up and go all the way to the library. Just sit down, dressed or not at all and start typing and move a mouse. Type in subjects or questions that you were too embarrassed to ask a librarian.

What a treasure chest of information!

Let me stop here for a moment to say "parts of this chapter is not for the very young of age.) This writing is for teenagers and older. However, in some European and Scandinavian countries, it is normal for everyone to come to the dinner table nude. Their children have seen it all and heard a lot. Even the juicy parts, do not surprise them. You be the judge of what your children should know and whether to remove this chapter. If you're sitting at the table undressed, be careful when using the gravy. Don't spill it on your lap. It would really hurt.

What I learned about the human body, what it looks like, how it functions, stimulating it and the corresponding responses was fascinating. I've covered what I've learned and my personal comments in my first book and so we now move on into Anatomy 102, Human Behavior.

When I was a teenager in the 1950's there were names vaguely referred to like Kinsey, Masters and Johnson and also a foreign book called the Kama Sutra which was forbidden. It is time to find out, learn what they were about and maybe learn from it.

First: Alfred Kinsey.

Alfred Kinsey was a very controversial man. Some claim that his statistics leaned a lot upon his personal sexual experiences. He had sex with fellow college staff members, both male and female, young assistants, prostitutes, prison inmates but later researchers later deleted them from his end results, the results came out the same. He delved into areas that were considered taboo in the 1950's. Filmed and personally developed sex movies of his assistants performing in the secrecy of his attic at night. He interviewed sex offenders (sex with children). He delved into sodomy and masturbation, words which are used today in more friendly phrases. Sodomy is now described as back siding, doggy style but a little higher. Masturbation is not a word to be ashamed to use. It is a natural stress relieving function.

He was a college professor with degrees in biology and psychology and a doctorate in anatomy from Harvard University. He is considered to be a biologist and zoologist, also an expert on insects. He was hired by the University of Indiana as a professor in biology. On top of his courses on biology, he got permission to teach a non-credit course on Marriage. Because of his reputed experiences, there were hundreds of applicants for the course. To top all this knowledge, he has 1 ½ years of college credits in general engineering prior to moving into biology and zoology.

Professor Kinsey and his helpers interviewed over 18,000 people including teachers, students, prison inmates, homosexual deviants and homosexuals. He wrote about observed orgasms of over 300 children from ages 5 months old to 14 years old, both male and female. It was rumored that he and his wife shared a male lover. He not only interviewed homosexuals and prisoners but personally traveled to Chicago to meet and participate in their sexual activities in a big city.

He founded the Kinsey Institute for research in 1947 and wrote a book called "Sexual Behavior in the Human Male". It immediately became a best seller in 1948. Using a grant from the Rockefeller Foundation to do research, he and his student helpers interviewed 6,000 females for his next best seller book called "Sexual Behavior in the Human Female" published in 1953. He died in 1956 but his books are still available.

Alfred Kinsey bypassed society's mores and taboos to interview and participate personally in sexual subjects that were not talked about (hush, hush) in the 1950's. He actually learned about all of it personally and wrote about all the sexual practices of men, women and even children.

Second: Masters and Johnson

Following in the footsteps of Alfred Kinsey came William Masters. Studies by the team of Masters and Johnson sounds like 2 scientific men doing research on a new medical field called "Sexual Responses to Stimulation, a part of the unknown field of Sexology".

In reality, they were a physician with a background in obstetrics, gynecology and bio chemistry and she was a college sociology student that he hired to help in interviewing and screening volunteers for paid lab testing. He became an Associate Professor of clinical obstetrics and gynecology at Washington University in St. Louis, Missouri. Receiving his grant from the United States Institute of Health, he began his research, recruited prostitutes but found them unsuitable since they weren't normal sexual people like you and I. At the time, they knew and performed all of the sexual preferences of their customers including being back sided and also riding cowgirl style.

This wasn't the usual labs that we go to. We give blood, urine samples or get hooked up to an MRI or EKG or Ultrasound machine.

This was a Sexology Lab. Masters intended to study human sexual stimulation using measuring technology on live volunteers in a lab.

You were randomly teamed with a woman with both of you hooked up to machines and you masturbated separately, then together, you had sexual intercourse with her. I don't think they performed fellatio or cunnilingus. The machines (electroencephalographs, electrocardiographs) recorded your responses and you were filmed in color cinematography. Biochemical tests were also run. A man and a woman with clipboards in hand "Masters and Johnson" watched your responses. I imagine that it would be a little hard to perform but the study went on for 11 years and things got easier because none of the volunteers quit. 382 women and 312 men were hired for the lab study, ages ranged from 18 to 89 years old. Chemical changes in your body were recorded as you were stimulated, got aroused, reached full arousal and had an orgasm then relaxed. The women did not relax, they had multiple orgasms. The time period for men between ejaculations was 3-4 hours. Your rhythmic contractions throughout this cycle were recorded as well as filmed and observed by Masters and Johnson.

You probably did not want to go home and say to mom: "look ma, I'm in movies and I'm the star", for fear that she would ask you to tell her in detail exactly what you did, lest both of you got excited and moved into taboo acts. This was back in the late 50's and early 60's. Today, she might say "where do I sign up".

Based on the data that they collected, they wrote 2 top best seller books named "Human Sexual Response" in 1966 and "Human Sexual Inadequacy" in 1970. Their laboratory research proved that masturbation is ok, it is good for you. Stimulating your clitoris produces a strong orgasm equal to that felt in intercourse.

Other researchers later showed that the 2 orgasms were equally strong but of another type with different responses. Both equally satisfying.

They got married in 1971 to live happily ever after. The marriage lasted for 21 years. They got divorced in 1992.

Their names stand alongside Dr. Kinsey as giant pioneers in the unexplored field of sexology.

Third: the Kama Sutra

Oh, Wow! Put on your seat belts, breath normally, there are pictures, 65 pictures and vivid descriptions of sexual positions.

In reality, the Kama Sutra is not a book of naughty, dirty sexual positions as we were led to believe. In Christianity, our belief is that God is love, he loves us no matter what. In India, their culture is God makes love. They celebrate life and attain pleasure by making love to both men and women, animals, objects. Whichever way that gives them pleasure. There are rules that guide them but not like our rules. Sex with other than your spouse is permitted, young siblings who have attained puberty is ok, homosexuality is not frowned upon, as long as both parties are in agreement. Of course, objects don't need permission. Objects like inflatable dolls, vibrators, dildos, masturbators, cucumbers, bananas, brush handles, dildos, etc. Even penetrating the anus is not forbidden. A woman sitting under an elephant is depicted in the Kama Sutra. Like I said to start with, this chapter does get juicy. As shown by the studies of Kinsey and Masters and Johnson, women's sexual needs are just as powerful as men's.

Kama (pleasure) does not conflict with Moksha (a religious life).

The 4 steps of life are Dharma, Arta, Kama and Moksha.

First you learn morals and ethics, then attain professional success, then, seek pleasure. Take pleasure from anything that pleases you. Music, art, sex, etc. Finally, seek liberating your soul by being a religious person.

The lessons you can adapt from the ancient Kama Sutra are to celebrate life by living it to its fullest, seek whatever interests you, others do other things. Do not argue about which way is right or better, try both ways, walk the middle if it pleases you, as long as it is not illegal. We have stringent rules to follow on what is illegal. Sex with youngsters who have reached puberty is illegal. Girls reach puberty at age 12 and boys at 14. Any sexual activity between adults and youngsters under the age of 18 is illegal. Sodomy among adults is frowned upon but not considered wrong.

Yes, we have many rules and regulations to follow. Families sitting around the house nude is not the norm but is no one else's business. Go out the door into the public naked is a punishable offense. You may go out into the public bra-less, show deep cleavages, go panty-less and wear high skirts or short dresses with slit sides is ok, briefly cross your legs for comfort is exciting but not an offense. How men react to it may lead to punishable offenses for him.

The Kama Sutra does contain sexual positions but is not a book about naughty sexual positions. It is about how to live a regulated, joyful life. The pursuit of pleasure and religion do not conflict.

B.   COMPUTERS

Atomic warfare is not a hush, hush secret anymore. We build bombers and missiles with the capability to carry nuclear bombs or warheads. Bombers carry bombs and missiles carry warheads. What good is it to travel thousands of miles to destroy just several blocks of a city. We have nuclear bombs and warheads that will destroy the entire city and the surrounding area.

If we are attacked, we will strike back with everything in our arsenal, an amazing amount of firepower. It will be all-out warfare with a massive amount of destruction on both sides. We are not talking about small countries like Iran, Afghanistan, Syria but major combatants who can destroy our country and our way of life. It has taken this long for the general public to slowly realize that we are vulnerable and not isolated from the rest of the world. Honor those of us who battle today or have battled to protect our way of life, do not put us down.

In 1969 and 1970, I was assigned to, first the Operations Section and later the Intelligence Section of a large triple F-4 Fighter Wing at Yokota AFB, Japan. One squadron rotated into South Korea to sit on nuclear alert. It was the Intelligence Sections job to construct and update target folders for the aircrews so they can reach their assigned targets and land at a designated airfield.

My friend and co-worker Chuck and I punched data cards with our flight plans on them for entry into the IBM computer in Hawaii. It was one of 4 giant IBM computers in the world. In 1969, computers were in their early stages of development. It was before transistors and later solid state memory and microchips. There were no personal laptops or desktops available not even tablets or readers. This large computer was located underground in the Alternate Pacific Command Center in rural Hawaii.

In a nuclear war, there would be bombers dropping nuclear bombs, missiles with nuclear warheads exploding, submarines firing missiles, fighters dropping bombs, every which way a nuclear warhead could be delivered, exploded on enemy territory. Chaos and mass confusion. The nuclear explosions send out shock waves for a determined amount of time and length as well as blinding flashes of light. Our fighters had to avoid being destroyed or our pilots flash blinded. The giant computer with inputs from all the commands, both Naval and Air force, integrated all the data and determined which of our own strikes had to be re-programmed.

Our Wing Commander sent an operations team consisting of Lt. Colonel Jack as leader and spokesman, and Chuck and I as experts and programmers inconspicuously on a commercial flight to Hawaii to attend this conference. We courier, transported our punch cards to the conference to be entered into the giant computer's program along with others. We spent almost a week at the conference correcting our flight plans and re-punching new computer cards. Data from the punched cards were transferred to magnetic tape and fed into the computer. Working besides Chuck, I became very fast at punching error free cards. With Jack as our leader, we became a very strong team. One day, while waiting for the others, Chuck and I wandered around the underground area. We stumbled into a large darkened office with the door wide open. It was the PACAF Commanders emergency office. 3 phones located on his desk, one labeled direct line to the Joint Chiefs of Staff. We hurried out of the office and went to find the small cafeteria manned by Navy cooks. Excellent breakfast, the cooks must have been hand selected because in case of an emergency, they had to feed Admirals and Generals.

Before the conference ended, we were taken to see the data room, location of the giant IBM computer. It was a large cylindrical heavy beast, probably weighing a ton with cables feeding it from tape decks lined up along 3 sides of the room.

In the past 20 years, I've watched several movies on TV that depicted a similar computer used in a small theater sized room with a wall sized screen in the front, desks facing it and the computer on the right side. Data was fed to it from a separate data room and the computer used to display second by second occurrences around the world or in a specified area. Like nuclear explosions in a nuclear war. Of course, they were just mockups for a movie with Hollywood speculating on what happened. All of this equipment is now obsolete.

In the 1960s and early 1970s, computers converted from using vacuum tubes to transistors and computer memory from magnetic core to solid state semi-conductor memory. That made all my magnetic tape decks obsolete and all the cassette tapes that I recorded for the new Buick Riviera we ordered for our return to the United States obsolete. By 1980, computers were air cooled, smaller and used commercially as well as in offices. We no longer needed the specially cooled mainframes of the old computer data centers.

The 1980s became the micro -computer era. The IBM PC computer was released. Apple was founded in the early 1980s. Every large electronic company was already in the field vying with their version of the home computer. CD ROM Drive was installed in almost all of the computers. Dell became the largest manufacturer until 2006 when Hewlett Packard (HP) replaced them by buying out Compaq in 2002 and inheriting smaller companies like Tandem and Digital Equipment. They exchanged the lead several times. Everything progressed rapidly to what we have today.

Laptops started in 1985 and looked like large sewing machines. You have to smile when it was called a laptop. They must mean portable enough to take home. We now have slim, portable designs you can comfortably fit onto your lap and put your fingers on its screen or peck away. We have I-Phones, tablets, readers all inter connectable, run by batteries.

It is hard to imagine what else they can dream up. I thought that we were a long way from seeing each other via phone or computer. It was always science fiction but surprise, surprise. Don't forget about the camera you purchased from Walmart for $35.00 to sit atop your desktop computer and turn on your Skype program to talk to someone with your vitals showing. Today, it takes 2 to tango. Both parties must be on the same frequencies but things change. They will probably build it into your computer and be a touch away. When you channel surf, you may accidentally be watched by your party talking to another party on another channel, like Facebook does to multiply their users into the billions.

I bought my first computer in 2009 to do research for my first book. It was an HP Vista. 5 years later, all the technicians say to keep it, it is a good computer. Any problems with using it does not mean that it is the computers fault. It can be corrected to run like new. I bought several books on how to use it but it was in a language that I didn't speak, Greek! (That is just an expression from the old days.) Finally, I bought a book written by Abby Stokes in a family oriented catalogue called "Is This

Thing On?" It guided me through understanding most of the basics. Niece Andrea patiently explained to me how to get photographs sent to others via the Picasa program and daughter Teresa took the time to get me through many stumbling blocks that I created and could not get out of my own mess. Thank you, thank you!

Hooray! I can now type in any subject or word and a list of web sites come up to look at. Some of them contain pictures and videos to watch, some are order catalogues that you can order from, etc. Amazon is a great site, you are able to read honest customer reviews, pro or con. It comes by 2 day shipping right to your door if you pay a reasonable yearly fee. Face book has become everyone's personal diary except it's not private anymore. No-one listens unless you personally address them by name. Everyone is busy trying to be clever or cute talking about their own interests. No "Howdy partner, what's up?" from anyone.

Like everyone else who uses a computer, you become hooked. Check all the email messages and delete all the ads, watch the current hot stories, check the weather every day. Even remember why you turned on the computer in the first place. At least the computer doesn't bug you like the constant ringing of your phone by telemarketers. You have to stop what you are doing and check the phone, it might be just someone that you know or an important personal call. You can sit down at the computer at your leisure, you have it under control. The time goes by so quickly. Duties and chores are overlooked. I must get up and catch up with today before it disappears into night.

C. MASSAGE

Massage looks like a very interesting and useful window to step through. It is an ancient art form used for many reasons. To relax tense muscles, treat injured or sore muscles, relax stressed muscles which happen when a mother gives birth. To reduce pain, joint stiffness, help improve one's circulation, reduce anxiety and depression, or stimulate the release of endorphins and serotonin, also improve sleep. Most clients of a professional massage therapist say that the go to them on a regular basis because it relaxes them and improves their life style. It is also used for sensual pleasure or excitement.

In the book of Ester, the wives of Xerxes took daily treatments daily using the oil of myrrh, meaning that it was rubbed on them.

Massage was used by nurses until the 1970s to ease patient's pain and to help them sleep. In Europe, nannies masturbated their male charges every night to help them sleep.

There are over 80 different types of massages, each with its own modal (method or rules).

Here in the U.S., you must be licensed to practice massage. Plus, each state, county, city, town has its own special restrictions.

Personally, I would prefer to be touched gently and smoothly, the Swedish massage would be a good place to start learning since it does just that.

Swedish Massage.

You begin by using a small amount of oil and spreading it over a selected area using the effleurage motion (using the pads of your finger tips or palm, touching and stroking the area with a smooth and light touch, also in a circular motion. This warms up all the muscles in the area and loosens them. You start the massage for any area to be worked on in the same way. A full body massage starts with the person laying down, face up on a padded massage table, undressed with a warm sheet covering all the body not to be worked on except the head and neck. The atmosphere is relaxed, calm with soothing music, no distractions, lights faced away from the person.

Standing at the head of the massage table, reach forward and effleurage the upper chest in a designated motion from the start of the cleavage, slowly up the sides of the neck, under the chin, around the jawbone up to the ears. Use sweeping motions across forehead, rub eyebrows and work your way into scalp. This relaxes the mind and helps ease tension and worries.

Next, stand on one side, work on one arm. Begin by spreading oil from the wrist up the arm to the top of the shoulder and back rubbing gently using a hand shake motion. Rub using your thumb and fingers. Now, flatten your hand and glide smoothly up and back several times. Work the top of the shoulder by squeezing in a movement from neck and around the shoulder bone. Move to the hand, knead each finger and glide up the arm to the elbow to move to working on the lower arm. Effleurage motions are used to move smoothly from working on one area to the next. Petrissage (kneading) the area from elbow to wrist by laying you hand flat and kneading by opening and closing your hand like doing handshakes. Finish massaging the arm by smoothing over the arm like you started. Move to the other side and repeat on the other arm.

Legs are next. My favorite area is the thighs, they excite me. Starting with one leg, spread oil with both hands, move up the leg to waist with one hand on the outside and to the crotch on the inside. Move hands smoothly up and back 3 to 4 times to warm the area. Next, rub the entire leg using a circular motion from toes to crotch. Squeeze the foot from either side, moving from heel to tip of toes and stroke back toward the heart with the palms of your hands. Now, work from vagina/penis down to ankle. Using both hands, one on either side of the leg, rub in circles moving slowly down to the toes. Finish by effleurage back up entire leg to vagina/penis in smooth strokes. Don't be embarrassed if you gently nudge the balls or rub up the outer side of the labia lips. Now, repeat on the other leg.

Have the person turn over toward you, then onto the stomach. Hold sheet up lengthwise and avoid looking or admiring. Work on the legs. Move the legs apart and smooth oil using both hands from toes to butt with smooth gliding motions. Now massage the bottom of the foot by grasping the foot on both sides and rub in a circular way, rub the inside bottom of foot.

This improves circulation and sexual stimulation of other body functions. Work on the toes, bottom of foot, around the heel and with smooth strokes, up to just below the crotch. Now use petrissage kneading and work up to crotch and back. Knead calf muscles and back of thighs with both hands. Finish by rubbing smoothly up and own leg. Next, repeat on the other leg.

Moving to the back, move to the head of the massage board and spread oil in long, stroking motions from the front to the back, over the entire back to the waistline. Massage neck and move down the back in circular strokes. This relieves sore and stiff muscles, improves skin texture and glandular functions. Use more oil, effleurage in smooth strokes up and down back, circular strokes around both sides and around shoulder muscles. Move to one side and apply deep kneading around the upper butt up to shoulder and top of arm. Up and down from spine to the side. Deep massage from top of butt to neck working on the shoulder and arm to the elbow. Smooth out the area and you're finished. The words effleurage and petrissage are French, not Swedish.

It is not really a full body massage since we've left out the face, breasts and buttocks which are massaged separately upon request.

My wife and partner broke her hip bone and is also suffering from a debilitating illness so I'm unable to practice massaging. I bought a massage table, different oils DVDs on how to do it, pads, etc. I was specifically hoping to help her regain her muscular strength but she has not improved enough to be able to handle a massage.

CHAPTER SIXTEEN

Reflections

My 4 children have grown up to be strong, independent personalities. They defend their beliefs and try to live by them.

Pam, Teresa and Ron have become my pillars of strength for me to lean against. They help me take care of Dorothy as she is slowly getting weaker. Bill lives and works in Los Angeles and cannot help but he keeps in touch with Pam and Ron often. I would crash without their help and not be able to even finish this book. I am proud of them.

The last 7 years have been a wild and many times lonely ride. Enjoyable. Sometimes sad, sometimes aggravating and sometimes down right sorry. I've had my share of disappointments, failures, successes. You eventually learn to take the bad along with the good.

Don't be a Chicken Little saying "The sky is falling!" Don't hide from it all. Live life to its fullest, enjoy living. Sometimes failures lead to a better understanding of life and its follies.

Lessons learned early in life are invaluable. They guide you through life and are a crutch to lean on when you are in trouble.

One lesson that I learned is to keep on trucking. Even though the odds are against you, if you see a glimmer of light ahead, press on. Somehow, some way, you will defeat the problem at hand. Working very long hours in the coffee fields gave me the mental strength to keep going when times got hard.

Another lesson is to try taking on 3 jobs or chores in the same time period. It could be an hour, half a day or a full day. If you get tired or are having problems accomplishing the first, move to the next. They could be anything. Housekeeping or yard work, maybe cutting a melon or writing a poem, anything. Stop before you get frustrated, just come back to it later.

At my age, taking a short nap in the afternoon is definitely one of the 3 happenings. When you finally get back to the problematic job, you will be refreshed and ready to attack it with maybe a new approach or at any rate, more patience.

Stop talking about your self-worth and listen while others speak. Give them a chance to express themselves. Experiences of others may add to your knowledge and be valuable. You waste a lot of time and energy thinking about how wrong they are. Make a friend by being a friend and listening to them.

We sometimes don't enjoy experiences when they happen and pass it off saying "I'll come back and do it later. Fully enjoy it when I have more time or money." I have never gone back to Paris, New York City to see the Statue of Liberty or the Empire State Building, never gone back to touch a glacier in Glacier State Park, went around the world with a partner, visited Maui or even did doggie exercises. But—there is still time to do some of it.

Reach out to others with your kindness. You may not have much to offer materially or physically but you have kindness and love. They are powerful tools to aid you in helping others. Help others and in turn they will help you.

Don't stop living a joyful life. Live in the present but look ahead and not backward. There are more things to learn, more places to see and definitely more joyful moments to fill your heart and memory.

I am still looking forward to improving my life. My stamina is gone so it must be back on the treadmill every day to regain some of it. I am trying to finish converting the walls of my greenhouse so it can be used as a weight training and exercise area to regain some of my strength using very light weights.

With more stamina and strength plus a stronger back, my performance should improve.

There is a third book to be written. It will be an adult book, fiction and erotic. My life is still moving forward.